She Will Do Him Good

A Study of God's Marvelous Design for the Wife

by Rosanne Surrett

Surrett Family Publications
Kings Mountain, NC

Copyright 2016

ISBN 978-0978933128

Acknowledgments

I want to thank my husband Chuck for his helps of encouragement, suggestions, additions, proofreading and "re-proofreading!" Without his help, I could never have finished the book. He has not only been a great help, but he has been a great husband. I am thankful for his testimony, patience, leadership, love, and faithfulness to me for so many years. He is my best friend and was my pastor for many years, for which I am very thankful.

The ladies of Dyer Baptist Church in Dyer, Indiana blessed me with their faithfulness and words of encouragement as I taught many of them some of these ideas in a "rough draft" form. We spent ten years studying the Bible together and serving in our church. A special thanks to Aletha Davis, who encouraged me to publish my work, to Mrs. Tammy Quinlan and my brother Steven Van Pelt who proofread my book, and to Mrs. Diane Hefner for designing the cover for my book. The ladies of Emmanuel Baptist Church in Kings Mountain, North Carolina have been a great blessing and encouragement also. It has been a joy and a privilege to serve with them since 1992. I am also thankful to Ambassador Baptist College for the privilege of teaching young ladies who have been a part of my "Help Meet" class.

I would like to dedicate this book to my mother, Mrs. Marjorie Van Pelt, who is with the Lord. I did not hear much spoken specifically about the virtuous woman while growing up. However, I observed one in my home–she was my mother. She truly was an "unselfish woman of strength, ability, and moral worth, who was different from the world, and very highly treasured." She was a beautiful lady, and she truly "did good" for her husband, my father. I am thankful to have had a mother who was an excellent example of a wife and mother.

- No part of this publication may be reproduced without the prior written permission of the author. When proper credit is given, quotations may be used.

- All Scripture verses are taken from the King James Version.

❦ About the Book

God declared, in Genesis 2:18, "It is not good that the man should be alone: I will make him an help meet for him." God then uniquely created the woman from the man, for the man–"for his good." In Proverbs 31, King Lemuel's mother counseled her son concerning finding the wife who would "do good" for him. She said that this woman would be more valuable than any earthly treasures he might ever obtain (v. 10), that he would be able to safely trust in her (v. 11), and that she would do "good for him, and not evil" all the days of her life (v. 12). He would be so pleased with her that he would declare her to be the greatest woman of all (v. 29)!

Join me in a study about the wife who "does good–and not evil" to and for her husband, all the days of her life. We will consider some examples of help meets who fulfilled their purpose–to do good for their husbands. We will also study examples of wives who had destructive influences on their husbands, thus failing to glorify God or to fulfill His purpose for their lives.

Determine to follow the example of Ruth, who honored her husband Mahlon, even after his death. She was no longer able to help Mahlon, but she certainly honored him with her testimony of godly character and unselfish service. She made a covenant of faithfulness to Naomi, her mother-in-law, for the remainder of her life. Her covenant of faithfulness was based on a commitment to God.

❦ To the Student

I want to share what I believe are God's plan and purpose for the woman, more specifically, the help meet. It is not an exhaustive study; I have much more to learn. My goal is to establish what I believe and teach on Scripture. However, my opinions are negotiable, although I try to establish them on Scripture also.

I hope you will learn much and make it your goal to honor the LORD by doing good to and for your husband, your best friend, each day of your life!

Rosanne Surrett, Proverbs 16:3

Contents

Chapter One - The "Hopeful" Help Meet's Choices - "Her Godly Determinations" 7
    Leadership Versus Dictatorship. 16
    Warning Signs of an Abusive Man. 17
    Ungodly Character Qualities of the Misogynist. 19

Chapter Two - The Help Meet's Marvelous Design - "For Him" 20

Chapter Three - The Help Meet's Majestic Worth - "Far Above Rubies" 27
    Suggestions for Personal Growth in God's Word. 34
    Your "Six Friends" in Bible Study. 36

Chapter Four - The Help Meet's Self-Motivation - "Working with Hands of Delight!" . . . 37
    "Shape Up" Your Home Management Skills. 44
    Eliminate the "Clutter". 51
    Meal Planning. 55
    Hints for Laundry Efficiency. 58
    Teaching Responsibility and its Benefits to Children. 60

Chapter Five - The Help Meet's Prudent Words - "As Choice Silver" 61

Chapter Six - The Help Meet's Meek and Quiet Spirit - "Of Great Price" 70

Chapter Seven - The Help Meet's Great Influence - "For Good, Not Evil!" 77

Chapter Eight - The Help Meet's Captivation - "Loving and Kind" 87

Chapter Nine - The Help Meet's Honorable Clothing - "Designed by God" 92

**Chapter Ten - The Help Meet's Ten Commandments - "Right Choices - Real
    Happiness"** 104

Works Cited 115

Notes 117

Chapter One

The "Hopeful" Help Meet's Choices - "Her Godly Determinations"

- ✦ Scripture: Proverbs 3:5-6
- ✦ Principle: Seek to obey God's Word, rather than search for a husband.
- ✦ Proverbs 3:5-6: "Trust in the Lord with all thine heart, and lean not unto thine own understanding; In all thy ways acknowledge him, and he shall direct thy paths."

Do you remember playing "wedding" when you were young? Someone said, "You be the bride . . . and I'll be the groom." Maybe you borrowed some of your mother's old dresses, picked up your dandelion bouquet, marched down the "aisle"–and lived "happily ever after"–for a few minutes. The next week you played the same game with a different groom. It did not really matter who was the groom. It was just for pretend–not for real.

I am sure you desire to someday walk down an aisle in your beautiful wedding gown, while the man who is to become your husband proudly smiles at you. Your vows during that very special and sacred ceremony will include the phrase, "Til death do us part." When you make that life-changing, life-long commitment, it is not wise to look around, find someone who is good-looking, says he is saved, and say, "Yes, I'll be your bride."

You see, you are a bride for a very short time–then you're a wife for life.

At the end of *that* ceremony you will not be pronounced "groom and bride." You will be pronounced "husband and wife," one flesh for life.

How can you be sure you are making the right decision, marrying the right man? It begins with *becoming* the right person, making the right *choices*. Then, if the Lord wills, He will bring the right man to you. You will be *doing good* for your husband *before* you marry him. *Prepare yourself to be a servant, and if the Lord wills, a help meet who will do good for your husband all the days of your life.*

Let's consider five choices you must make, in order to become and marry the "right person."

I. Determine to accept God's decision.
II. Determine to develop godly character.
III. Determine to submit to Biblical authority.
IV. Determine to serve–not to search.
V. Determine to evaluate your "potential" husband's character.

I. **Determine to accept God's decision.**

    A. Refuse to worry about it (Phil. 4:6a).

    B. Resolve to pray about it (Phil. 4:6b).

    C. Rest in the Lord about it (Phil. 4:7).

    D. Surrender your body to God (Rom. 12:1).
        1. *Beseech* means "to beg," "for that person's own good."[1]
        2. *Present* means "to place beside."[2]

    E. Refuse to be conformed to the world (Rom. 12:2).
        1. *Conform* means ". . . to fashion or shape one thing like another. . . ."[3]
        2. *Conform* has ". . . especial reference to that which is transitory, changeable, unstable. . . ."[4]
        3. *Conform* ". . . could not be used of inward transformation."[5]

✦ "The word rendered *conform* properly means to put on the 'form, fashion, or appearance of another. It may refer to anything pertaining to the habit, manner, dress, style of living, etc., of another.'"[6]

    F. Renew your mind daily (Rom. 12:2).
        1. *Renew* is " . . . the adjustment of the moral and spiritual vision and thinking to the mind of God, which is designed to have a transforming effect upon the life. . . ."[7]
        2. *Prove* is "'to test, prove,' with the expectation of approving. . . ."[8]
        3. Allow God to transform your life, as you adjust your thinking to the mind of God.
        4. As you let God transform your mind, He will reveal His perfect will.

    G. Application: _____

II. **Determine to develop Godly character.**

    A. Choose to remain pure (I Cor. 6:18-7:1; II Tim. 2:22).
        1. Run from fornication (I Cor. 6:18; II Tim 2:22).
            a. *Fornication* means ". . . illicit sexual intercourse."[9]
            b. Fornication is a sin against one's own body (I Cor. 6:18).
        2. Do not make provision ("forethought") for the flesh (Rom. 13:14).[10]
            a. Determine to have a no touch relationship with the opposite sex (I Cor. 7:1).

Determine to remain pure. Defilement will likely occur without a prior commitment to purity. The higher degree of purity you desire, the greater abhorrence of defilement you will have. (Daniel 1:8)

   b. Determine to not flirt with your eyes (Prov. 6:25).
   c. Determine to not tantalize men's passions with immodest dress, because men are aroused by sight (I Tim. 2:9-10).

- "Personal apparel represents deliberate choices and is a guide to personality. How we dress . . . shows sexual attraction and sexual interest, group identification, status, identification of role, and expression of self-concept."[11]
- You cannot dress in a worldly manner and then be offended if people think you are worldly.

   (1) Modest apparel is "orderly, well-arranged, decent, modest . . . in its primary sense as 'harmonious arrangement, adornment. . . .'"[12]

- This is a modesty in the sense of "orderliness." It should be in agreement with your profession of godliness.

   (2) Shamefacedness
   ". . . a sense of shame, modesty . . . having regard to others, respectfulness,
   . . . modesty which is rooted in character,
   . . . would always restrain a good man from an unworthy act."[13]

- As a godly woman, you must show respect through your dress to God and your male head, who is either your father if you are unmarried or your husband if you are married. When selecting clothing to purchase or to wear, ask yourself, "Does this garment show respect to God and to my father or my husband? Will it bring them shame? Will it cause any man to have sensual thoughts?" Determine to *honor God* with your dress–not arouse the *passions* of a man.
- This is modesty in the sense of "respectfulness."

Your clothing must enhance your profession of godliness.

   (3) Sobriety is ". . . soundness of mind . . . 'sound judgment' practically expresses the meaning. . . ."[14]

- This is modesty in the sense of "self-control."

   (4) Not with gold or pearls or costly array

- *Costly array* means "primarily, 'the very end or limit'. . . with reference to price, of highest 'cost,' very expensive . . . raiment. . . . (I Tim. 2:9)"[15]
- The inner meek and quiet spirit is, in God's sight, of great price (I Pet. 3:4). The Greek word used for *costly array* (I Tim. 2:9) in regard to the *outward apparel* is the same word used for *great price* (I Pet. 3:4) in regard to the *inner meek and quiet spirit*. In both I Timothy and I Peter God discourages the wearing of very expensive clothing. In I Timothy women are exhorted to let their outward adornment be modest–not costly–accompanied by good works. In I Peter, God commands the development of an inner meek and quiet spirit, which is extremely valuable in God's sight. We must regard very highly what *God* declares to be "of the highest cost," not what *man* regards most valuable.
- A godly woman's spirit–not her clothing–should be "of great price."

                (5) Feminine (Deut. 22:5-12)
                (6) Distinguished by good works, not external decorations, which support your profession of godliness
            d. Establish dress guidelines based on Scripture (I Cor. 10:31).
✦ If your nonverbal communication disagrees with your verbal communication, people tend to believe that your nonverbal is the most valid. Therefore, if you profess a testimony of salvation, but you dress in a sensual manner, people will tend to believe that you have a sensual, not a spiritual focus. They may even assume you are not saved.
                (1) Long enough to cover your thighs at all times (Gen. 3:21; Ex. 28:42; Is. 47:1-3)
                (2) High enough so your breasts are not exposed or undue attention is called to that area of your body
                (3) Loose enough so your breasts are not emphasized
✦ Godly men should not have to focus solely on your face to keep their thoughts pure. Ungodly men will not even bother to try to focus only on your face.
        3. Realize your body belongs to God–not yourself (I Cor. 6:19-20).
            a. Your body is borrowed (v. 19).
                (1) Your body, which is permanently indwelt by the Holy Ghost, belongs to God (v. 19).
                (2) Your body will belong to your future husband, if God gives you a husband (I Cor. 7:4).
            b. Your body has been purchased with Jesus' blood (v. 20; Acts 20:28).
✦ When a Christian woman keeps back and uses for herself what belongs to God, she is stealing from God.
        4. Glorify God with your body (I Cor. 6:20).
        5. Refrain from being "available" (Gen. 2:18-22; 3:16).
            a. God knew Adam was alone, which was not good (Gen. 2:18).
            b. God knew Adam needed a helper (Gen. 2:20).
            c. God made Eve (Gen. 2:21-22a).
            d. God brought Eve to Adam (Gen. 2:22b).
            e. God commanded Eve to desire Adam (Gen. 3:16).
            f. God told Eve that Adam would rule her (Gen. 3:16).

    B. Choose to develop prudence.
        1. *Prudence* is the ability to reason wisely, speak correctly, and live godly.
        2. Prudence is contrasted with simplicity, which " . . . might relate to the immature or simple one who is open to all kinds of enticement, not having developed discriminating judgment as to right and wrong. . . ."[16]
        3. Prudence is acquired–not inherited.
            a. You must have a relationship with the Lord (Prov. 19:14).
            b. You must have a humble spirit, willing to accept reproof (Prov. 15:5).
            c. You must study God's Word (Ps. 19:7; Prov. 1:4-5; 18:15).
            d. You must apply God's Word (Prov. 1:4; James 1:25).
        4. Prudence is contrasted with simplicity in Proverbs.

C. Application: _____
_____

III. **Determine to submit to legitimate authority.**

   A. Submit to Biblical authority.
      1. Parental authority (Eph. 6:1)
      2. Spiritual authority (Heb. 13:17)
      3. Civil authority (Rom. 13:1)

   B. Be aware of the consequences of rebellion against Biblical authority (I Sam. 8).
      1. Rejection of the authority over you is rejection of God's authority (v. 7).
      2. God allows you to reject His authority (v. 7).
      3. Rejection of God's authority brings bondage (vv. 9-18).
      4. Rejection of God's authority will cost you much more than you can foresee (vv. 9-18).
      5. God sometimes says, "I will give you what you want, but you must live with the consequences (vv. 7-18)."

   C. Reject ungodly advice (Ps. 1:1). See "Warning Signs of an Abusive Man."
      1. Walk not in the counsel of the ungodly (Ps. 1:1).
      2. Make no friendship with an angry man (Prov. 22:24-25).
         a. You must not be with him (v. 24).
         b. You will become like him (v. 25).
         c. You will be trapped (v. 25).
         d. You will experience much strife (Prov. 29:22).
      3. Reject the unbiblical and unreasonable demands of exclusive loyalty to a "boyfriend."
         a. The virtuous woman, who was married, carried on business with merchants, probably male merchants (Prov. 31:24).
         b. Abigail, Nabal's prudent wife, appealed to David in the presence of four hundred soldiers (I Sam. 25:23-31).
         c. Lydia, a new believer, invited Paul, Silas, and Timothy to lodge at her house (Acts 16:1-15).
         d. Two sisters, Mary and Martha, entertained Jesus in their home (Lk. 10:38-42).
      4. If you are in a relationship with an abusive man, you must end it immediately and completely!

   D. Application: _____
   _____

IV. **Determine to serve–not to search.**

    A. Focus on serving others–not seeking your own satisfaction.
- Though just a child, Samuel said, ". . . Speak, for thy servant heareth (I Sam. 3:10)."
- A servant concentrates on obeying his master's commands. If you have a servant's heart, you can complete any legitimate, assigned task, with the Lord's help.

    B. Develop Biblical habits.
        1. Establish Biblical priorities (Matt. 6:33).
        2. Esteem others better than yourself (Phil. 2:3).
        3. Use carefully the time God has given you (Ps. 90:12; Eph. 5:16).
- Number your days and redeem the time God gives you. Opportunities to make wise choices cannot be recalled if missed. Opportunities become regrets if you make wrong choices.
- Purchase a planner or use a small notebook and make up your own "planner pages."

        4. Value and organize the possessions God has given you (Prov. 12:27).
- Organization of your belongings will save you much time and frustration. Have a place for everything and put everything in its place.

        5. Diligently complete assignments on time, doing your best with the gifts God has given you (Col. 3:23).
        6. Budget the finances God has given you; give to the Lord first (Prov. 3:9).
        7. Identify your areas of weakness, areas in which you lack knowledge, skill, or motivation (Mt. 26:41; Mk. 14:38; John 15:5; Ph. 4:13).
        8. Work on your weaknesses one at a time, depending on the Lord for wisdom and strength (Phil. 4:13; James 1:5).
- Begin with your most important area of weakness.

        9. When you have completed a task, ask yourself the following question. "Would the Lord say, 'Well done, thou good and faithful servant?'" (Matt. 25:21, 23)
        10. Memorize and apply I Corinthians 10:31. "Whether therefore ye eat or drink, or whatsoever ye do, do all to the glory of God."

    C. Follow the example of two women who chose to diligently, unselfishly serve others, rather than search for husbands.
        1. Who were they?
            a. Rebekah, a single woman, chose to serve her family and a stranger (Gen. 24:15-67).
            b. Ruth, a widow, chose to serve her mother-in-law, Naomi (Ruth 1-4).
        2. What were their character qualities?

Rebekah (Genesis 24:15-67)	**Ruth (Ruth 1-4)**
Virgin (v. 16)	Honorable widow of Mahlon (4:10)
Was in the right place (vv. 11-13)	Assumed the right place (1:16-17)
Found fulfilling responsibility (vv. 13-15)	Assumed responsibility (2:2-11)
Generous (v. 18)	Kind (1:8)
Servant's heart (vv. 19-20, 46)	Servant's heart (2:2)
Obedient to authority (vv. 51, 58)	Obedient to authority (1:16-17; 2:21-23; 3:5)
Self-motivated, unselfish worker (vv. 17-20)	Self-motivated, unselfish worker (2:2)

Diligent worker (v. 20)   Diligent worker (2:7, 11, 14)
                                            Loyal, "clave to Naomi," (1:14)
Steadfast (v. 58)   Steadfast (1:18)
Protected her testimony (v. 61)   Established and maintained a good testimony
                                               (3:11)

      3. What did God do for them?
         a. God brought a servant, who represented her future husband, to Rebekah (Gen. 24).
         b. God brought a redeemer (husband) to Ruth (Ruth 2:3; 4:10, 13).
         c. God brought both women into the lineage of Christ (Matt. 1:5)

  D. Application: _____
_____

V. Determine to Scripturally evaluate your "potential" husband's character.

  A. Ask the following questions about the man you are evaluating:

Question	Yes	No	Scripture
1. Does he shew evidence of true salvation?			II Cor. 6:14
2. Could he be your spiritual leader?			I Cor. 11:3
3. Does he have the approval of your parents?			Eph. 6:2
4. Are his goals and values Christ-honoring?			Matt. 6:33
5. Does he make decisions based on Biblical principles?			Col. 3:15; Phil. 2:13
6. Is he a faithful, serving member of a fundamental local church?			Heb. 10:25
7. Is he financially responsible?			Luke 16:10
8. Is he a diligent worker, willing to complete assigned tasks?			Gen. 3:19
9. Does he honor and obey his parents and other Biblical authorities?			Eph. 6:1-2; Rom. 13:1
10. Is he a peace maker-or an angry man with a short fuse?			Prov. 22:24-25 James 3:14-16
11. Is he willing to accept and to learn from correction?			Prov. 15:5
12. Does he admit when he is wrong or does he make excuses?			I John 1:9
13. Does he demand your submission to his "authority"?			Eph. 5:22
14. Is he honest?			Ex. 20:16
15. Does he break the rules when no one is watching?			Num. 32:23

16. Does he think he is the "exception to the rules"?			Rom. 13:1-2
17. Does he practice Biblical principles in regard to finances?			Prov. 3:9-10
18. What is his final authority for faith and practice–God's Word or his word?			II Tim. 3:16

  B. Test his professed love.
    1. The Scripture Test
      a. Read I Corinthians 13 where godly love is defined.
      b. Substitute his name for the word *love* in verses 4-7.
      c. Result? He passes. _____ He fails. _____

    2. The Logic Test
      In deductive reasoning, when one has a positive premise and a negative premise, the conclusion must be negative.
        True love suffers long and is kind.
      _____ (his name) suffers long and is kind.
          Or
      _____ (his name) does *not* suffer long and is *not* kind.
      Therefore, _____ (his name) does love
          Or
      _____ (his name) does not love!

Remember, you must become the right person in order to marry the right person!
✦ Determine to accept God's decision and God's timing.
    Do not worry about it, but determine to pray about it and rest in the Lord.
    Surrender your body to God.
    Refuse to be conformed to the world, and renew your mind daily.
✦ Determine to develop godly character and prudence.
    Remain pure.
    Set Biblical standards for what you will wear and do.
    Accept correction with humility in order to develop prudence.
    Do not be easily available.
✦ Determine to submit to Biblical authority.
    Spiritual authority
    Parental authority
    Civil authority
    Reject illegitimate "authority."
✦ Determine to serve–not to search.
    Focus on serving others, rather than seeking your own satisfaction.
    Develop Biblical work habits.
✦ Determine to Scripturally evaluate your "potential" husband's character.
    Test his professed love Scripturally.
    Test his professed love logically.

Prepare yourself to be a servant. Seek to *obey* God's Word, rather than to *search* for a husband (Proverbs 3:5-6). You must determine to choose wisely now, in order to best prepare yourself to do good for your future husband, as the Lord wills.

Suppose you have already violated some of the principles in this chapter. First, confess your sin to the Lord, no matter what sins that may involve. God has promised to forgive and cleanse you, not just from some sins, but He has promised ". . . to forgive us our sins, and to cleanse us from all unrighteousness (I John 1:9)."

God blessed Boaz with a very special place in history. His *mother* Rahab had been a former harlot, who became a believer in Jehovah, and had an important role in Israel's victory over Jericho. Boaz's *wife*, Ruth, had been a heathen woman who became a believer in Jehovah. God placed both women, Rahab and Ruth, in the lineage of Christ. Truly, He is a merciful and gracious God.

When Ruth entered Bethlehem, she was called the Moabitish damsel. Approximately four months later, the entire city acknowledged that she was a virtuous woman.

Second, review the Five Determinations above; make a personal commitment to the Lord to follow each one. Flee temptation when it comes! Then, rest in the Lord concerning your forgiveness and cleansing from sin, and His choice of a husband for you. Determine to read God's Word daily and memorize Scripture. Let God's Word strengthen and guide you. You can still be a "hopeful help meet"–just put your hope in the Lord. Determine to serve others, not to search for a husband!

Develop your homemaking skills. Learn to cook. Collect recipes from your mother and other family members; get recipes for your favorite foods which they make. Put the recipes into a photo album (in the photo slots), which will keep them clean. Learn the basics of sewing. Even if you do not use that skill to make clothing, you could use it make basic curtains, pillows, etc., to decorate your home more economically. Write up a budget by which you should live right now and live on it. Developing that discipline will be invaluable later. Make sure you know how to do basic house cleaning; you will need that skill for sure! Begin to organize your possessions now when you have a limited amount of "stuff!" Set priorities and determine to follow them as much as possible. And remember, you must become the right person in order to marry the right person.

✦ I am making the following decisions, based upon Scripture:

_____
_____
_____
_____
_____
_____

Leadership versus Dictatorship

Paul versus Nabal and Rehoboam

I Thess. 2:5-8; I Sam. 25:10-17; I Kings 12:13-15

Dr. Charles L. Surrett

	Leader	Dictator
Goals	Edify followers	Gratify self
Motives	Glorify God	Make name for self
Treatment of others	Loving and gentle	Harsh and cruel
Personal discipline	Tough on self	Self-indulgent
View of self	Servant	Master
View of others	Precious	Expendable
Leadership style	Example	Command
Mode of operation	Uses work to build people	Uses people to build work
If success comes	Gives credit	Takes credit
If failure comes	Takes blame	Assigns blame
Result in followers	Want to work	Have to work
How others see him	Beloved	Hated

Warning Signs of an Abusive Man
(*Misogynist* - "Woman hater")

The abusive man's goal is **total control**; his weapons are his **words and moods**.

1. A push for quick involvement

2. Jealousy

3. Controlling
    + In every conflict in the relationship the man must win and the woman must lose!

4. Unrealistic expectations

5. Isolation

6. Blames others for all his mistakes

7. Makes everyone else responsible for his feelings

8. Hypersensitivity

9. Cruelty to animals and children

10. "Playful" use of force during sex

11. Verbal abuse

12. Rigid sex roles

13. Sudden mood swings
    + "An angry man stirreth up strife, and a furious man aboundeth in transgression (Prov. 29:22)."
    + "As long as anger lives, she continues to be the mother of many unhappy children."[17]

14. Past battering

15. Threats of violence
    + Warning signs one through fifteen used by permission from *Today's Christian Woman*, Jan/Feb,1996, 43-46, Sherri Langton.[18]

16. Subtle manipulation[19]

Ungodly Character Qualities of the Misogynist

Characteristics of Misogynist	Scriptures Violated
He does not love the woman.	I Jn. 3:18: "... Let us not love in word, neither in tongue; but in deed and in truth."
The unmarried man strives to control the woman. The husband strives to control every aspect of his wife's life.	Eph. 6:1: "Children obey your parents...." Eph. 5:22-25: The wife is to submit to her husband; the husband is to love his wife.
He yells, threatens, strikes, and displays anger–all of which are evidences of a proud spirit. (Prov. 13:10)	Eph. 4:31: "Let all bitterness, and wrath, and anger... be put away from you...."
He shifts the blame for all wrongs to his partner.	I Jn. 1:9; Prov. 28:13: Without confession of sin there is no forgiveness from God.
He seeks oneness *before* marriage.	Gen. 2:24: Eve became a wife *before* she became one with Adam physically.
He refuses to submit to any authority who disagrees with him; then, he falsely discredits that authority.	Rom. 13:1: "Let every soul be subject unto the higher powers...." II Tim. 3:3: "... not false accusers...."
He demands that the woman love him and give to him.	Eph. 5:25: Husbands are to love their wives as Christ loved and gave Himself for the church.
The wife is to be tower of strength; the husband is a demanding infant.	Eph. 5:23: The husband is to nourish his wife.
The man abuses and tears down the woman until she is almost incapable of effectiveness.	Eph. 4:29: Communication should edify–not corrupt. Prov. 31:10-31: The wife is commended by God as a very productive and efficient helper.
The man denies incidents and reshapes them.	Ex. 20:16: "Thou shalt not bear false witness against thy neighbor."
The man narrows the woman's world; he demands that she focus only on him and his needs.	Prov. 31:10-31: Her husband is her priority, but she helps others.
The woman fears the man.	II Tim. 1:7: "For God hath not given us the spirit of fear ...." I Jn. 4:18: "There is no fear in love, but perfect love casteth out fear...."
He is a liar and a hypocrite.	I Jn. 1:6: "If we say we have fellowship with him, and walk in darkness, we lie and do not the truth."
He uses harsh, bitter words. He disparages others' character and wounds their feelings.	I Pet. 2:23: "Who (Christ) when he was reviled, reviled not again...." See I Cor. 6:10.
He is extremely jealous, which results in strife, confusion, and every evil work! (James 3:14-16)	James 3:14-18: The truly wise man exhibits peace, gentleness, mercy, can be easily entreated, does not exhibit partiality or hypocrisy, but makes peace.
He exhibits the fruit of the flesh. (Gal. 5:19-21) (See Warning Sign #13 - Violent Mood Swings)	Gal. 5:22-23: He must exhibit the fruit of the Spirit.

Chapter Two

The Help Meet's Marvelous Design - "For Him"

- ✦ Scripture: Genesis 2:18-25
- ✦ Principle: God uniquely designed the help meet for her husband.
- ✦ Genesis 2:18: "And the LORD God said, 'It is not good that the man should be alone; I will make him an help meet for him.'"

How can one make proper use of an object unless one knows the designers' purpose for that object? Its purpose is best known by its creator and designer. A rolling pin was not designed to mix a cake, nor was a mixer designed to roll out pie dough. When utensils are used properly, the results are much more desirable.

God created everything in order, with purpose and with perfection (Genesis 1-2). He uniquely designed and created Eve to be a helper, completer, and companion *for* Adam. Among all the things that God made in the six days of Creation, this was the only time the Hebrew word *banah* was used. The word is translated *made*, which means "build." The woman was uniquely *taken from* Adam, *built for* Adam, and *brought to* Adam–all for his *good*.

Nothing else in creation quite matches the woman's unique creation.

Adam had food to eat (Genesis 2:9,16) and a perfect environment (Genesis 1:31). He had the privilege of God's presence, guidance, and instruction (Genesis 2:15-17). God gave Adam a job to do (Genesis 2:15). Adam was endowed with great intelligence and authority, in that he named all the animals. Whatever name Adam gave to an animal, that was its name (Genesis 2:19-20). However, God declared that it was not good for Adam to be alone. From Adam God took a rib and "built" Eve. God decided that it was better for Adam to be without one of his ribs than to be alone. If God knows that one truly needs something, He can give it to her/him for her/his good.

As a help meet fulfills her God-given purposes, she is most useful and successful. Some women consider themselves highly valuable, while belittling their family and home responsibilities. They conclude that they must work outside the home, to fulfill *their* view of their self-worth. A woman's estimations of herself and her responsibility(ies) reveal *her* values and determine *her* choices.

All Creation obeyed God's designated plan for them, with the exception of two groups of beings–angels and man. A woman has only one acceptable response to God's purpose for her. "Let me be what I was made to be–let me be a woman."[20] If she is blessed with a husband, she must say, "I will become the helper to my husband that God uniquely designed me to be. I will do it for God's glory and for my husband's good." Obedience to God is evidence of one's high regard for the Authority of His Word. God does not take lightly disobedience to His Word (I Samuel 15:22-23). *A wife must choose to do good–not evil–for her husband each day of her life.*

I. What is the definition of a help meet?
II. Why did God create the help meet?
III. How did God design the help meet?
IV. How did Eve respond to God's design for her as a help meet?
V. How should a help meet respond to God's design for her?

I. What is the definition of a help meet?

    A. A help meet is a wife who was uniquely designed by God to fulfill her husband's needs as his helper, completer, and companion (Gen. 2:18).
        1. The word for *help meet* is *ezer*, which means "help, support, helper."[21]
        2. The word denotes "assistance," but it more frequently refers to the "assistant."[22]
        3. The same word is used of God as man's help or helper forty-two times in the Old Testament.
        4. The Almighty God is willing to help His Creation; therefore, a wife should highly esteem, not disdain, her position as a helper to her husband.

    B. A help meet was designed to be that virtuous woman of Proverbs 31, an unselfish woman of strength, ability, and moral worth, who is different from the world and highly-treasured (Prov. 31:10-31).

    C. Application: _____
_____

II. Why did God create the help meet?

    A. She was created for the glory of God (Is. 43:7; Rev. 4:11).

    B. She was created for the good of her husband (Gen. 2:18).
- "She will do him good and not evil all the days of her life (Prov. 31:12)." The word *do* means "deal fully with, recompense."[23] In their commentary, Jamieson, Fausset, and Brown suggest the idea of "contributing good to him," citing Abigail as an example of such a wife.[24]
- We are commanded to "Withhold not good from them to whom it is due, when it is in the power of thine hand to do it. Say not unto thy neighbour, 'Go, and come again, and to morrow I will give;' when thou hast it by thee (Prov. 3:27-28)."
- The word *neighbor* means "friend, companion, fellow, another person."[25]

This command would surely demand that a wife not withhold-but rather gladly do that which benefits her husband-the one for whose welfare she was created.

          1. She was created to help her husband, for his good (Gen. 2:18).
✦ One's title indicates one's responsibilities. A teacher teaches, a fireman fights fires, a waitress waits on customers, and a helper helps. Therefore, a *help* meet's responsibility is to *help* her husband. A wife who does not fulfill her title is not fulfilling her responsibility. She *is* a wife, but she *is not* a help meet.
          2. She was created to complete her husband, for his good (Gen. 2:20-24).
          3. She was created to be a companion to her husband, for his good (Gen. 2:18).

    C. Application: _____
_____

III. How did God design the help meet? Genesis 2:20-24

    A. God formed her body from a rib of Adam's body (v. 21).
        1. God created Eve from Adam, not Adam from Eve (vv. 22-23; I Cor. 11:8).
            a. God formed (*yatsar*) Adam from the dust of the ground (v. 7).[26]
            b. God made (*banah* -"built") Eve from one of Adam's ribs (v. 22).[27]
✦ God's order and manner in which He created Adam and Eve display His design for their purposes: Adam, the leader of his wife and Eve, a helper to her husband.
        2. God created Eve for Adam–not Adam for Eve (vv. 22-23; I Cor. 11:9).
        3. God designed Eve to be different from Adam.
        4. God designed Eve's body to complete Adam's body (vv. 20-24).

    B. God established her relationship as his wife to be permanent (v. 24; Mk. 10:2-9).

    C. God established her position as a helper to her husband, the ruler (Gen. 3:16).
        1. In the Creation, Adam was formed first (Gen. 2:7-8, 15-18; I Tim. 2:13).
        2. In the Fall, Eve was deceived (Gen. 3:13; I Tim. 2:14).

    D. God established her responsibilities to her husband.
        1. She was to be his helper (v. 18).
        2. She was to be his completer, willing to satisfy him physically (vv. 20-24) and to bare his children (1:28; 3:16).
        3. She was to be his companion (v. 18), desiring and loving him (3:16).

    E. God allowed Adam to name Eve (vv. 22-24; 3:20).

    F. God commanded Adam and Eve to leave their parents and cleave to each other (v. 24).

    G. Application: _____
_____

IV. How did Eve respond to God's design for her as a help meet?

    A. Eve understood God's instructions concerning eating of the tree of the knowledge of good and evil.
        1. She knew what God allowed them to eat (Gen. 2:16; 3:1-2).
        2. She knew what God had forbidden them to eat (Gen. 2:17; 3:3).
        3. She knew the consequence for disobedience to God's Word (Gen. 2:17; 3:3).

    B. Eve mishandled God's Word.
        1. She should have ended the conversation when Satan questioned God's Word (Gen. 3:1).
        2. She omitted God's Words which indicated her great freedom (Gen. 2:16; 3:2).
        3. She added words which emphasized her one restriction (Gen 2:17; 3:3).

A choice to misuse God's Word results in failure and punishment!

    C. Eve was deceived by Satan (Gen. 3:1-6; I Tim. 2:14).
        1. She believed Satan's lie about the results of eating of the tree (vv. 5-6).
            a. God said, ". . . In the day that thou eatest thereof, thou shalt surely die (Gen. 2:17)."
            b. Satan said, " . . . Ye shall not surely die. For God doth know that in the day ye eat thereof, then your eyes shall be opened, and ye shall be as gods, knowing good and evil (vv. 4-5)."
            c. Satan quoted some of God's words, but not all of God's words.
            d. Satan outright denied God's Word.

A choice to believe and act upon false teaching will result in harmful consequences!

✦   Eve found out too late that God's Word is always true; Satan is always a liar.
        2. She was not content to accept the position God had given her (vv. 5-6).
        3. She thought the tree offered her something better than what God had given her (v. 6).
            a. God had given her unbroken fellowship with Him.
            b. God had given her a perfect husband (Gen. 1:31).
            c. God had given her a perfect marriage.
            d. God had given her perfect environment (Gen. 1:31).
            e. God had given her the ability to bear children (Gen. 1:28).
            f. God had given her a clear conscience (Gen. 1:31).

    D. Eve succumbed to Satan's temptation.
        1. ". . . Ye shall be as gods, knowing good and evil Gen. 3:5)."
        2. Eve was created in God's image, knowing good (Gen. 1:27, 31).
        3. Eve did not need to know evil.

            a. Some knowledge is better left unknown (Rom. 16:19).
            b. Some knowledge acquired results in a burden.
        4. Eve chose to take the fruit, eat it, and give it to Adam (Gen. 3:6).

    E. Eve's sin was the result of pride (Is. 14:12-15).
        1. Lucifer was not content with the position God had given him (v. 13).
        2. Lucifer wanted to be like God (v. 14).

Discontentment–if not dealt with–leads to more sin!

        3. Pride results in destruction (v. 12; Prov. 16:18).

    F. Adam and Eve suffered consequences for their sin (Gen. 3:7-24).

How long did it take Eve to eat and enjoy the fruit?
It was insignificant in relation to the irreversible,
dreadful consequences which followed.

        1. Eve knew the consequence for her sin; however, she did not know the extent of the consequence (Gen. 4:3-12).
        2. Adam was influenced to sin (v. 17).
        3. Sin entered the world because of Adam's sin (Rom. 5:12).
        4. Death for all mankind was the punishment for sin (v. 19; Rom. 5:12).
        5. Adam and Eve lost their clear consciences.
            a. They knew shame–they tried to cover their bodies (v. 7).
            b. They felt guilt–they tried to hide from God (v. 8).
        6. Adam and Eve lost their unbroken fellowship with God (vv. 8-10).
        7. They felt fear–they tried to hide from God.
        8. Adam and Eve lost their oneness–Adam blamed Eve (v. 12).
        9. The serpent was cursed (v. 14; Is. 14:12-15).
        10. Eve would have sorrow in the childbearing process (v. 16).
        11. The ground was cursed (vv. 17-18).
        12. *Toil* ("hard work involving sweat") would be needed to make the earth fruitful (vv. 18-19). *Dressing* ("working") it would no longer be sufficient (2:15).
        13. Adam and Eve knew evil, but it was not good, like everything God had made (v. 22).
        14. Adam and Eve lost their perfect environment (vv. 22-24).

Authority was instituted for man's protection–not for his punishment.

        15. God promised a Savior for their sin (v. 15) and provided clothing to cover their nakedness (v. 21).

G. Application: _____

V. How should a help meet respond to God's design for her?

A. A help meet must choose to submit to God's plan for her life.
 1. Mary accepted God's plan for her (Lk. 1:38), which resulted in good.
    a. Mary's choice was the result of a humble spirit.
    b. Mary was content with God's plan for her.

Mary accepted God's Word and was highly praised (Lk. 1:42, 48).

    c. Mary experienced joy in the birth of her child, the Savior, whose death provides life for all who believe in Him.
 2. Eve rejected God's plan for her (Gen. 3:6) and did evil to Adam.
    a. Eve's choice was the result of pride.
    b. Eve was not content with God's plan for her.

Eve "walked in the counsel of the ungodly" and paid a great price (Gen. 3:6-24).

    c. Eve experienced sorrow during the birth of her sons, who experienced death as the result of their father Adam's sin.

B. A help meet's choice to accept God's design fulfills her purposes.
 1. God is glorified (Rev. 4:11).
 2. Her husband's needs are met as she does good to and for him (Prov. 31:10-12).
    a. She helps her husband (Gen. 2:18).
    b. She completes her husband (Gen. 2:20-24).
    c. She is a companion to her husband (Gen. 2:18).

C. A help meet's choice to obey God's design brings rewards (Prov. 31:25, 28-31).
 1. She is happy (John 13:17).
 2. She is blessed by her children (Prov. 31:28).
    a. The word for *blessed* is *asher*.
    b. *Blessed* is a word:
       (1) reserved for a man to bless another man,
       (2) used of envious desire,
       (3) used of congratulation,
       (4) that indicates that the blessing is earned.[28]
 3. She is praised by her husband (Prov. 31:28-29).
    a. The word for *praise* is *halal*.[29]
    b. He trusts in her, because she has met his needs (Prov. 31:11).
    c. He receives good–not evil–from her (Prov. 31:12).

       d. He considers her superior:
          "... Her price is far above rubies (Prov. 31:10)."
          "... Thou excellest them all (Prov. 31:29)."
    4. She is praised by her works (Prov. 31:31).
    5. She is free, the result of obedience (John 8:32).

"The special gift and ability of each creature defines its special limitations . . . the woman who accepts the limitations of womanhood finds in those very limitations her gifts, her special calling-wings, in fact, which bear her up into perfect freedom, into the will of God."[30]

Elisabeth Elliot

    D. Application: _____
_____

    A help meet is a wife who was uniquely designed by God to help, complete, and to be a companion to her husband, in order to fulfill his needs. As she recognizes and joyfully accepts God's special design for her as a helper, she fulfills her husband's needs and her purpose in life. She does not have to strive to become someone that she was not designed to be. She herself is the recipient of joy, blessing, and freedom. The ultimate result is that God is glorified in her life. *She does good for her husband!*

    Have you recognized and accepted God's special design for you as a helper? As a single woman, you were designed to help others. As a wife, you must make a conscious choice to help, complete, and to be a companion to your husband. You must choose to do "good" and not "evil" to him and for him–all the days of your life!

Rejection of God's design harms both the husband and his wife!
1. Husband influenced to sin (Gen. 3:17)
2. Sorrow in childbearing (Gen. 3:16)
3. Criticism from her husband (Gen. 3:12)
4. Separation from God (Gen. 3:8)
5. A rebuke from God (Gen. 3:16)
6. Bondage (Jude 6)

Acceptance of God's design benefits both the husband and his wife!
1. Husband's needs are met (Prov. 31:11)
2. Praise from her children (Prov. 31:28)
3. Praise from her husband (Prov. 31:28-29)
4. Fellowship with God (Gen. 2:8, 15-17)
5. Praise from God (Prov. 31:30)
6. Freedom (John 8:32)

✦   **You must accept God's specific design for you as given in His Word!**

Are you just a wife–or are you truly a help meet?

Chapter Three

The Help Meet's Majestic Worth - "Far Above Rubies"

- Scripture: Proverbs 31:10-12; Ruth 1-4
- Principle: A wife must be a virtuous woman to be of great value to her husband.
- Proverbs 31:10: "Who can find a virtuous woman? for her price is far above rubies."

A help meet is a wife who was uniquely designed by God to fulfill her husband's needs as his helper, completer, and companion (Genesis 2:18).

Since man's loneliness was the only circumstance in all creation pronounced "not good," then a help meet must be of great value to her husband.

However, how does a man find this extremely valuable woman? That very question was asked by King Lemuel's mother thousands of years ago. It is still being pondered today. Many men have a wife, but the man who has a help meet is the one who is blessed indeed. *His wife strives to do good for him–each day of her life!*

Several years ago my husband surveyed some married couples in a local church. It was disturbing to learn that the husbands were evenly divided as to whether or not Christian women made better wives. Some husbands even answered, "No." It was revealing to note that the percentage of husbands who said Christian women were better wives was almost identical to the percentage of the wives who consistently spent time in God's Word.

Elisabeth Elliot said, "The fact that I am a woman does not make me a different kind of a Christian, but the fact that I am a Christian does make me a different kind of a woman."[31] Since God's Word states that a virtuous woman's value is far above rubies, let's consider what It teaches concerning the virtuous woman. *She will do good for her husband–all the days of her life!*

I. What is God's definition of a virtuous woman?
II. Who was an example of a virtuous woman?
III. How can one become a virtuous woman?
IV. What effect does a virtuous woman have on her husband?

I. What is God's definition of a virtuous woman? Proverbs 31:10-31

    A. God's Word defines her as a woman of strength, ability, and moral worth (v. 10).
        1. She is strong (v. 17)–yet meek (I Pet. 3:1-6).
            a. She is meek, an evidence of strength–not *weakness*.
            b. She has physical strength to work–not just to have a *beautiful body*.
            c. She has mental strength; she continues to learn.
            d. She has emotional strength to make decisions based on Biblical principles–not on *emotions*.
            e. She gains spiritual strength through growth in her knowledge of God and the application of His Word.
            f. She has strength of character:
                (1) strength of resolve–to do good for her husband (v. 12).
                (2) strength of service–to work willingly and sacrificially (v. 13).
                (3) strength to spend and invest her money wisely (vv. 16, 24).
                (4) strength of restraint, speaking kindly and wisely (v. 26).
                (5) strength of maturity–helping the poor and needy who cannot repay her kindnesses (v. 20).
        2. She has the ability to serve (vv. 11-27).
            a. The *virtuous woman* means a "woman of ability" (Prov. 12:4; 31:10, 29; Ruth 3:11).
            b. She is able to diligently, unselfishly serve others (vv. 11-27).
                (1) She serves her husband, her first earthly priority (vv. 11-12).
                (2) She serves her family, her second priority (vv. 13-27).
                      Fulfilling priorities requires maturity.
                      Inability to put others first indicates that one is not ready for marriage!
                      Doing for others while neglecting one's family is wrong!
                (3) She serves others, the poor and needy (v. 20; II Kings 4:8-10).
                (4) She considers her needs, which are important, but not her first priority (vv. 17, 22, 25).
        3. She has moral worth (v. 30), in contrast to the strange woman (Prov. 2:16-17; 5:3-6; 7:5-23).
            a. The virtuous woman fears the Lord, which established her moral worth (Prov. 31:30).

✦ "Above all, she fears the Lord. Beauty recommends none to God, nor is it a proof of wisdom and goodness, but it has deceived many a man who made his choice of a wife by it. But the fear of God reigning in the heart, is the beauty of the soul; it lasts forever."[32]

            b. The strange woman is rebellious toward God, destitute of moral worth (Prov. 2:16-17).
            c. The evidence of the virtuous woman's moral worth is her unselfish concern for others (Prov. 31:13-27).
            d. The evidence of the strange woman's lack of moral worth is her selfish concern for herself (Prov. 7:10-21).

e. The virtuous woman does good for others (Prov. 31:11-27).
f. The strange woman does evil to others (Prov. 2:18-19; 7:26-27).

A wife can perform her duties and yet not truly fulfill the needs of her family. Her spirit is of great importance! She should be a better wife because she is a Christian. Only a virtuous woman has the resources to unselfishly and continually serve others.

B. God's Word states that the virtuous woman is rare (v. 10).
 1. She is difficult to find.
 2. She is different from most women, unaffected by worldly philosophy when determining her direction and values.
 3. She makes wise choices which set her apart.
    a. She chooses God's Word–not humanism, as her authority (Acts 5:29).
    b. She chooses to be modest–which is not considered fashionable (I Tim. 2:9-10).
    c. She chooses to be submissive–which is considered old-fashioned (Eph. 5:22).
    d. She chooses Biblical priorities (husband, family, and home, if she is married), before a career (Prov. 31:27).
    e. She chooses to be unselfish–"You first"–not "Me first" or "I'm worth it!" (Prov. 31:11-27)

C. God's Word states that the virtuous woman is highly-treasured (v. 10).
 1. Her worth is far above rubies!
 2. Her worth is comparable to wisdom's worth (Prov. 8:11).
 3. Her worth is measured by her influence on others.

D. Therefore, the virtuous woman is an unselfish woman of strength, ability, and moral worth, who is different from the world and highly-treasured.

E. Application: _____
_____

II. Who was an example of a virtuous woman? Ruth 1-4

A. Ruth was one of the few women in the Bible called a virtuous woman (Ruth 3:11).
 1. Ruth became virtuous in God's sight through salvation (1:16).
 2. Ruth established a testimony of virtuous character in man's sight.
    a. A servant recognized her strength (2:7).
    b. Boaz recognized her ability to serve (2:11).
    c. Boaz recognized her moral worth (3:11).

*When Ruth entered the gates of Bethlehem, she was known as
the Moabitish damsel (2:6).
Approximately four months later, she was known as
a virtuous woman (3:11).*

   3. Ruth established a testimony of being virtuous in man's sight by her diligent, unselfish service for Naomi (2:11-12; 3:11).
      a. Ruth gave up her family and ambitions and chose to spend her life with Naomi, her mother-in-law (1:16-17; 2:11).
         (1) Intreat me not to leave thee,
         (2) whither thou goest, I will go,
         (3) where thou lodgest, I will lodge,
         (4) thy people shall be my people.
            Orpah had said she would return with Naomi to her people (1:10).
            Orpah returned to her own people (1:15).
         (5) and thy God my God.
            Orpah had not made a commitment to Naomi's god.
            Orpah returned to her gods (1:15).

Without a true commitment to God, a commitment to a person is more likely to be broken.

            Ruth had promised to return with Naomi to her people (1:10).
            Ruth had recognized just one God–Jehovah–and He became her God (1:16).

A commitment to a person, based upon a true commitment to God, is more likely to endure.

         (6) where thou diest, will I die.

Certainly one could not be any more loyal to someone than Ruth was to Naomi!

      b. Ruth chose to remain a widow and childless.
      c. Ruth chose to serve Naomi (2:2-7).
         (1) Ruth served someone other than herself, an indication of her unselfishness.
         (2) Ruth worked as a gleaner, an indication of her humility (2:2).
         (3) Ruth worked diligently, an evidence of her self-motivation (2:7).
         (4) Ruth worked unselfishly to fulfill Naomi's needs.
            Physical needs (2:11-12)

Companionship needs (2:23; 4:15)
(5) Ruth ". . . dwelt with her mother-in-law (2:23)."
(6) Ruth loved her mother-in-law (4:15).

B. Ruth was blessed by God as she served others.
1. Ruth was blessed with a husband (4:10).
2. Ruth was blessed with a son (4:13).
3. Ruth was brought into the lineage of Christ (Matt. 1:5).
   a. Rahab and Ruth were both mentioned in Christ's lineage, though neither was an Israelite.
      (1) Each one became a believer in Jehovah prior to her marriage.
      (2) Each one married a Hebrew man.
   b. Rahab married Salmon and was Boaz's mother (Ruth 4:21).
      (1) She was a Canaanite woman from Jericho (Josh. 2:1-15).
      (2) She was a former harlot (Josh. 2:1).
      (3) She declared her faith in Jehovah (Josh. 2:11).
      (4) She is commended as of a woman of faith, who did not perish with unbelievers (Heb. 11:31).
      (5) She identified with God's people (Josh. 6:25).
      (6) She validated her faith in by her works (James 2:25).
   c. Ruth became Boaz's wife and David's great-grandmother (4:22).
      (1) She was a Moabite woman (Ruth 1:4).
      (2) She declared her faith in God (Ruth 1:16).
      (3) She was commended by Boaz for her faith and works (Ruth 2:11-12).
      (4) She identified with God's people (Ruth 1:16).
      (5) She validated her faith by her works (Ruth 2:16; 3:11).
   d. God is a merciful and gracious God.
4. Ruth's story was recorded in God's Sacred Word.

C. Application: _____
_____
_____

III. How can you become a virtuous woman?

A. You become virtuous in God's sight through salvation (Eph. 2:8-9).
1. You must acknowledge that you are a sinner (Rom. 3:23).
2. You must believe that Jesus Christ died for your sins and rose from the dead (Rom. 10:9).
3. You must call upon Him, trusting Him alone to save you from sin (Rom. 10:13).

Your relationship with Christ is not the result of your birth or background, but it is the result of your new birth by faith in Jesus Christ. After salvation, you must establish a testimony of godliness for others to observe.

    B. You become virtuous in man's sight in two ways.
        1. You must have testimony of godly character (Ruth 3:11).
        2. You must have a testimony of unselfish service for others (Ruth 2:11-12; 3:11; Prov. 31:13-31; Eph. 2:10).

    C. Your testimony of salvation must be validated by your lifestyle.

    D. Application: _____
_____
_____

IV. What effect does a virtuous woman have on her husband?

    A. She is more valuable than any earthly riches that he may obtain (Prov. 31:10).

    B. She gives him a sense of security by fulfilling his needs (Prov. 31:11).

    C. She does good–not evil–for him, all the days of her life (Prov. 31:12).

    D. She helps him (Gen. 2:18; Prov. 31:10-12).

    E. She completes him (Gen. 2:20-24; Prov. 31:10-12).

    F. She is his companion, his best friend (Gen. 2:18; Prov. 31:10-12).

    G. She honors–not shames–him (Prov. 12:4; 31:23).

    H. Application: _____
_____

    A virtuous woman is of great value to her husband (Proverbs 31:10). Ruth was an example of that virtuous woman, who trusted in God, gave up her own personal desires, and determined to serve Naomi, her mother-in-law. As she did this, God blessed her with a godly husband, a son, and a place in the lineage of Christ.
    Ruth was extremely valuable, not only to Naomi, but also to Boaz. He received the gift of a virtuous woman, who was diligent and unselfish, a helper, completer, and companion–a true help meet. Boaz and Ruth must have had a blessed marriage. They were both unselfish, willing to put others' needs before their own needs.

*Ruth believed it was more important for her to care for Naomi's needs
than to seek her own satisfaction.
Boaz considered it more important for him to obey God's Word
than to retain his own inheritance.
They were both faithful to duty and to the vows they made.*

Salvation is the means by which you become *virtuous in God's sight* (Titus 3:5). However, you can be saved, and yet not appear virtuous in man's sight. Man can only observe your works–he cannot see your heart. If you establish a testimony as a woman with a servant's heart and godly character, you will become *virtuous in man's sight*.

A self-centered wife is concerned about *her own needs*. Because her usefulness is limited to herself, she is of little value. A virtuous woman is concerned about the *needs of others*. Because her unselfish service affects so many lives, she is extremely valuable. Her willingness to serve will cost her much, but she will be of great value to her husband, and to others. She should do good for her husband all the days of *her* life. Those days may even include her life prior to their marriage. They should include the days during their marriage, and after their marriage ends, if she outlives her husband.

As a wife, are your activities centered primarily around your own interests–or are you genuinely motivated to serve your husband and others? Are you doing good or evil to your husband, each day of your life? If you have failed in some way to do good for your husband, confess it to the Lord and your husband. Make a determination to do good for him.

Consider the following questions.
- Have I become virtuous in God's sight? _____
- Do I have a testimony of virtuous character and unselfish service? _____
- If not, what changes must I make? _____
  _____
  _____

- Whose needs should I be primarily concerned about if I am married? _____
- What character quality should summarize my life? _____
- In order to serve others unselfishly, I will:

_____
_____
_____

Suggestions for Personal Growth in God's Word

Be a woman of Bible study and prayer! Here are some ideas to help you grow spiritually through your personal Bible study. There is a blessing to those who daily hear God's Word and anticipate learning from it. (Proverbs 8:34)

- Have a journal to record what you learn.
- Pray, "Open thou mine eyes, that I may behold wondrous things out of thy law (Ps. 119:18)."
- Read slowly and deliberately one paragraph at a time.
- Ask yourself the following questions, suggested in *Our Daily Bread*.
    1. Is there an example for me to follow?
    2. Is there a sin for me to avoid?
    3. Is there a command for me to obey?
    4. Is there a promise for me to claim?
    5. Is there a principle to instruct me?

  A *principle* is "a fundamental truth or proposition serving as the foundation for belief or action."

    6. What can I learn about God? (Suggested by the author)
- Make an application for yourself. Write in your journal the Bible reference, the date, and something you learned that day. Make the passage a prayer or project.
- Save your completed journals for future review and reference.

Example: Read Proverbs 3:5-6. Ask yourself questions one through six.

1. Is there an example for me to follow?
    - None

2. Is there a sin for me to avoid?
    - I must not support (lean on) myself with my own finite, incomplete understanding.

3. Is there a command for me to obey?
    - I must trust in the Lord with *all* my heart.

Safely trust (*batach*) means "to trust," and ". . . expresses that sense of well-being and security which results from having something or someone in whom to place confidence . . . stressing the feeling of being safe and secure."[33]

- I must acknowledge the Lord in *all* my ways.

Knowledge means to "know" by (1) observing and reflection, and (2) experiencing.[34]

Somewhat characteristically the heart plays an important role in knowing. Because they experienced the sustaining presence of God during the wilderness wandering, the Israelites 'knew' in their hearts that God was disciplining or caring for them as a father cares for a son (Deut. 8:5). Such knowing can be hindered by a wrongly disposed heart (Ps. 95:10).[35]

4. Is there a promise for me to claim?
- ✦ My God will direct my paths if I know Him and trust in Him.

Direct (*yashar*) means "'to make (a way) straight' i.e. *(sic)* direct and level and free from obstacles, as when preparing to receive a royal visitor."[36]

5. Is there a principle to instruct me?
- ✦ Trusting in the Lord gives me security.
- ✦ Trusting in the Lord assures me that He will direct my paths.

6. What does my God do for me?
- ✦ My God directs my path and gives me security when I trust Him.

✦ Have a notebook for prayer requests and answers to prayer.

✦ The following book is suggested to help you in your study of the Bible. *An Expository Dictionary of Biblical Words*, by W. E. Vine, Merrill F. Unger, and William White, Jr., published in Nashville, TN, by Thomas Nelson Publishers in 1985.

✦ Download Online Bible from the internet.

Your "Six Friends" in Bible Study

Dr. Charles L. Surrett

- ✦ Use the following to enhance your study and application of God's Word.
- ✦ Sample study: Psalm 1:1-6

- ✦ **Who?**
    1. Who is the writer/speaker?
    2. Who are the readers/hearers?
    3. Who are the characters of the passage?
    4. To whom does it apply today?

- ✦ **What?**
    1. Is there a command to be obeyed?
    2. Is there a central lesson to be learned?
    3. What is the theme of the passage?
    4. What is the context all about?
    5. What application can be made to life today?

- ✦ **When?**
    1. Does the historical setting affect either interpretation or application?
    2. When must the commandment be obeyed?
    3. When will the consequences be realized?
    4. Is it a temporary idea or eternal principle?

- ✦ **Where?**
    1. Does the location of events affect interpretation or application?
    2. Does it have local or universal meaning?

- ✦ **How?**
    1. If a command, by what means can it be obeyed?
    2. What power and resources are available?

- ✦ **Why?**
    1. What motives should accompany obedience?
    2. What consequences will accompany obedience/disobedience?

Chapter Four

The Help Meet's Self-Motivation - "Working with Hands of Delight!"

- ✦ Scripture: Proverbs 31:13-27; 6:6-8
- ✦ Principle: A help meet must be a diligent helper, in order to be a godly homemaker.
- ✦ Proverbs 31:13: "She seeketh wool, and flax, and worketh willingly with her hands."

A help meet is a wife who, at Creation, was uniquely designed by God to help her husband. Her responsibilities were expanded in the Book of Wisdom and reinforced in the writings to the early Church.

A help meet is a homemaker, not a housewife. She is not the "wife of a house." The successful homemaker views herself as a helper. As she willingly accepts God's unique design for her and diligently fulfills her responsibilities, she becomes a homemaker. She builds up her family as she serves them and manages her home with "hands of delight!" An integral part of her success is her self-motivation. *Self-motivation is acting correctly to fulfill one's purpose, need, or desire, or the needs and desires of others.* A homemaker's self-motivation is directed as God designed–a helper to her husband and a godly mother to her children.

God has assigned the wife as manager–not president–of the most important company in the world. The hours are long, which is unacceptable to unions. The pay is set up on the installment plan: joys now, in the future, and in Heaven above.

As a wife, you have already accepted this position. Have you accepted the responsibilities and limitations of this management position?

How well are you managing this little corporation which God has entrusted to you? Are you seeking ways to shape up your skills and consequently improve your productivity, or do you seek ways to skip out of your responsibilities? As a single woman, do you cut corners, fail to attend to responsibilities? If so, you are lacking two very important character qualities which are necessary for becoming a godly homemaker: acceptance of responsibility and self-motivation!

Let's consider some ways to help you strengthen your motivation and improve your skills.
I. What is the definition of a homemaker?
II. What are the Biblical responsibilities of a homemaker?
III. What are some principles concerning diligence?
IV. What are the attitudes of a godly homemaker?
V. What are the results of diligence and laziness?

I. What is the definition of a homemaker?

   A. Webster's dictionary defines *homemaker* as "one who manages a household especially as a wife and mother."[37]

   B. God's Word declares that "Every wise woman buildeth her house, but the foolish plucketh it down with her hands (Prov. 14:1)."
      1. *Build* means "to build, establish, construct, rebuild."[38]
      2. "Metaphorically or figuratively, the verb *banah* is used to mean 'building one's house'–i.e., (sic) having children."[39]
      3. *House* means both "house and household."[40]
      4. A godly homemaker is a wise help meet who builds up her family as she wisely manages her home and fulfills her God-given responsibilities.

   ✦ Elijah Kellogg said, "Home is the place where character is built, where sacrifices to contribute to the happiness of others are made, and where love has taken up its abode."[41]

   C. Application: _____
   _____

II. What are the Biblical responsibilities of a homemaker? Proverbs 31:11-27

   A. Her responsibilities were established by God in His Word, not by man or woman.
      1. At Creation, the wife was created to be a helper (Gen. 2:18).
      2. In Proverbs, the wife was commended for being a diligent, virtuous helper (31:10-27).
      3. In the New Testament, the wife was instructed to be a keeper at home (Titus 2:3-5; I Tim. 5:14).
      4. The Biblical role of the wife has remained the same.

   B. Her responsibilities as a helper were given to the wife, not the husband.

   C. Her responsibilities should not be changed by the husband or his wife, since God established them.

   D. Her responsibilities must be fulfilled according to Biblical priorities.
      1. The Lord: She must fellowship with Him (Ps. 5:3; Matt. 6:33; Luke 10:38-42).
      2. Her husband: She must fulfill his needs (Prov. 31:11) and honor him (Prov. 31:23).
         a. She must help her husband (Gen. 2:18; Prov. 31:11-12).
         b. She must complete her husband (Gen. 2:20-24).
         c. She must be a companion to her husband; she must love him and desire to be with him (Gen. 2:18; Titus 2:4).
      3. Her family
         a. She must diligently feed her family (Prov. 31:14-16).

        b. She must clothe her family for all seasons (Prov. 31:13, 19, 21-22).
        c. She must guide and guard her home, taking care of every need (Prov. 31:27; Titus 2:5).
        d. She must assign tasks to those under her care (Prov. 31:15).
        e. She must value and carefully use her possessions (Prov. 31).
            (1) The field was for food and possible profit (vv. 14-16).
            (2) The fabric, such as wool and flax (from which linen was produced) was for clothing (vv. 13, 21-22), and for profit (v. 24).
    4. Herself (Prov. 31)
        a. Her strength must be used to work for the benefit of others, not just to display her physical attractiveness (v. 17).
        b. Her clothing should be elegant and attractive, not sloppy or sensual (vv. 22, 25).
        c. Her words must be spoken carefully with wisdom and kindness, not hastily with foolishness and hurtfulness (v. 26).
        d. Her work must be diligent; she must not waste time as a sluggard (v. 27).
    5. Her outreach
        a. She must help others by outreach and by example.
        b. She must reach out to the poor and needy (Prov. 31:20).
        c. She must teach, by example, the younger women Biblical priorities (Titus 2:3-5):
            (1) to love and honor their husbands,
            (2) to love and care for their families,
            (3) to care for their homes,
            (4) how to develop godly character.

E. She must wisely use her time, possessions, and words.

F. Her responsibilities must be summarized as serving others willingly while maintaining Biblical priorities.

G. Application: _____
_____

III. What are some principles concerning diligence?

A. *Diligence*, in the Scripture, has the idea of being determined, and refers to something which cannot be changed.[42]

B. *Diligent* is defined as "characterized by steady, earnest, and energetic application and effort."[43]

C. Diligence is demonstrated by the ant (Prov. 6:6-8).
   1. The ant is exceedingly wise (Prov. 10:5; 30:24-25).
   2. The ant accepts personal responsibility without coercion (v. 6).
   3. The ant is self-motivated, needing no overseer or ruler (v. 7).
   4. The ant is organized, fulfilling responsibilities according to priorities (v. 8).
      a. Gathers food steadily, little by little
      b. Provides (furnishes) food in the summer
      c. Gathers food in the harvest when the weather is right and food is available
   5. The ant is rewarded (v. 8).

D. Diligence is rewarded (Prov. 10:4b; 31:28-31; Mt. 25:14-30).
   1. Jesus told a parable about three servants to whom were given one, two, and five talents (v. 15).
   2. The master left for a time, returned, and demanded an account from each servant (v. 19).
   3. The faithful servants were commended for faithfulness over a few things (vv. 21, 23).
   4. The diligent servants were given greater authority (vv. 21, 23; Prov. 28:20).
   5. The unfaithful servant had the wrong attitude (vv. 24-25).
      a. He refused to accept personal responsibility, a character weakness.
      b. He blamed his master's character, a character weakness.
      c. He excused his failure to increase his talent, a character weakness.
   6. The unfaithful servant lost his talent and was punished (vv. 28-30).

E. Diligence is contrasted with slothfulness, defined as laziness, which is the result of wrong attitudes (Prov. 6:9-11).
   1. The sluggard was commanded to learn from the ant (Prov. 6:6).

✦ Sluggard: Prov. 6:6-11; 10:26; 13:4; 20:4; 26:16
✦ Slothful: Prov. 12:24, 27; 18:9; 19:24; 21:25-26; 22:13; 24:30-34; 26:13-15

   2. The sluggard refuses to accept personal responsibility, which is a character weakness (vv. 9-10; 19:24; 20:4; 21:25)!
   3. The sluggard is not self-motivated to work, which is a character weakness!
      a. Her priority is to overindulge in sleep, not in work (6:9)!
      b. She folds her hands in sleep–she does not use them to work (24:33)!
   4. The sluggard refuses to work, which is a character weakness (v. 9; 21:25)!
   5. The sluggard is not sacrificial, a character weakness (v. 9; 20:4)!
      a. She gives excuses why she cannot work (20:4).
      b. She always blames someone or something for her laziness.
   6. The slothful woman wastes the resources she has (12:27; 18:9).
   7. The sluggard receives poverty, which is her just reward (v. 11; 20:4).
      a. The sluggard has done no work, so she deserves no pay!
      b. The sluggard's poverty comes little by little.

c. The wicked does not regard the condition of the poor (Prov. 29:7); the sluggard becomes poor (Prov. 10:4a).
8. The sluggard is faced with unnecessary concern for the future (Prov. 20:4; 31:21).
9. The slothful woman covets things, but she will not work for them (Prov. 21:25-26).
10. The slothful woman is tempted to gossip with her mouth, because she is not working with her hands (II Thess. 3:11).
11. The slothful woman should not anticipate God's help, because God helps the poor and needy, not the sluggard (Ps. 113:7).

F. Productivity is not based on one's size or talent, i.e., the ant verses the sloth, but on the quality of one's character (Prov. 30:24-25).

G. Application: _____

IV. What are the attitudes of a godly homemaker? Proverbs 31

A. She accepts personal responsibility (Gen. 2:18-24; Prov. 31:11-27).

B. She is a self-motivated worker (v. 13).
1. The verbs describing her work are active verbs.
2. The diligent woman seeks work.
3. The diligent woman does not need an overseer.

C. She is a willing worker (v. 13; Ps. 40:8).
1. She must work voluntarily to fulfil her responsibilities assigned by God in His Word.
2. She must not work with a begrudging spirit, which is the evidence of carnality (Lk. 10:38-42).
    a. Martha no doubt was diligent, but she had the wrong priority, which was serving (vv. 40-41).
        (1) Martha received Jesus into her home (v. 38).
        (2) Martha's wrong priority resulted in the wrong attitude toward her service (v. 40).
        (3) Martha questioned the Lord's concern for her (v. 40).
        (4) Martha demanded Jesus change her circumstances (v. 40).
        (5) Martha had the wrong attitude toward Mary.
        (6) Martha was gently reprimanded by the Lord about her wrong priority and attitude (v. 41).
        (7) People may have benefitted from Martha's service, but they were probably uncomfortable with her attitude.
    b. Mary chose the highest priority (v. 42).

                (1) Mary received Jesus' words which will not pass away.
                (2) Mary did not condemn or argue with Martha.
                (3) Mary was commended by the Lord for her choice.
                (4) Mary also washed Jesus' feet (Jn. 11:2; 12:3).
            c. Worship and work are both commanded and commended, but they must be done in the proper order.

Spiritual growth is not the result of serving-but of the study and application of the Word of God.

   D. She is a sacrificial worker (v. 15).
      1. She serves her family at the expense of her own inconvenience.
      2. She serves those who cannot repay her generosity (v. 20).
         a. She is concerned with people, not possessions.
         b. She is able to give to those in need (Prov. 21:26).
         c. She obeys God's instructions (Deut. 15:1-11).
         d. She reaches out to the needy; they need not reach out to her.
         e. She validates her virtue by her actions, because "The righteous considereth the cause of the poor (Prov. 29:7. . . ."; cf Ps. 40:17). (*sic.*)

   E. She is a sober worker.
      1. She is of a sound mind and takes seriously the responsibilities assigned to her by God (Titus 2:4).
      2. She carefully watches over her family (Prov. 27:23).

   F. She is a careful worker, because she values her resources (Prov. 12:27).
      1. Her resources are carefully evaluated and used (Prov. 27:23-26).
      2. Her resources handled wisely can supply her needs and the needs of others (Prov. 27:18, 26-27).

   G. She is a thankful worker (Prov. 17:22; Phil. 4:4; I Thess. 5:18).

   H. She plans purposeful activity and purposeful inactivity.

   I. Application: _____
      _____

V. What are the results of diligence and laziness? Proverbs

   A. Diligence and slothfulness bring contrasting results, based upon one's focus.

| *The diligent focuses on others, which results in:* | *The lazy focuses on self, which results in:* |

profit (10:4),	poverty (10:4),
greater authority (12:24),	less authority (12:24),
building of her home (14:1),	destruction of her home (14:1); Eccl. 10:18),
satisfaction (20:13).	self-destruction (21:25).

    B. The diligent wife honors her husband (31:23).

    C. The diligent wife is praised by her husband (31:28-29).

    D. The diligent wife is praised by her Lord (31:30).

    E. The diligent wife is praised by her works (31:31; Titus 2:5).

✦ The works of her hands praise her in the gates. The poor and needy may be some of those people whom she willingly reached out to help.

    F. Application: _____
_____

    A godly homemaker is a wise help meet who builds up her family as she wisely and skillfully manages her home and fulfills her God-given responsibilities. She must be self-motivated to accomplish the responsibilities given to her in God's Word. She cannot depend on her mother, her husband, or anyone else to motivate her to accomplish her tasks–or to do them for her. She must work willingly, keeping her priorities and her attitude correct. Her family will be enriched by her influence and accomplishments.

    As a wife, have you accepted your responsibility to be a diligent homemaker, a home builder? Is your home in order? Is that little "company" that God has given you to manage suffering loss? If so, confess your failure as sin. Spend time evaluating your responsibilities and determine how to improve your productivity. Ask God to help you *set* Scriptural priorities. Ask Him to enable you to *fulfill* your priorities, not with drudgery–but with "hands of delight!" Determine to do good–not evil–to and for your husband, each day of your life.

If you begin your day with the Lord by choosing that better part,
which cannot be taken away, it will help you serve with a better–not a bitter–spirit.

"Shape Up" Your Home Management Skills

I. "Shape Up" your schedule.

    A. Discipline yourself to get up early in the morning (Prov. 31:15).
- In her book *Beautiful in God's Eyes,* Elizabeth George gives some benefits and ideas for early rising.
    1. Consider the benefits of rising early.
        a. Time alone
        b. Time alone with God
        c. Time to plan
        d. Time to get the jump on the day
    2. Consider some ideas on how to get up early.
        a. Determine a time to get up.
        b. Get to bed earlier.
        c. Say a prayer.
        d. Get up.[44]
- I would like to add thank God for another day!

    B. Purchase a notebook or planner.
- I designed my own planner page because I could not find one that fit my lifestyle. I print it and put it in my planner.

    C. Establish and write down Biblical priorities (Prov. 31:10-31).
1. Lord (Matt. 6:33)
2. Husband (Prov. 31:11-12)
3. Family (Prov. 31:13-19, 21, 23, 26-27)
4. Others (Prov. 31:20)
5. Yourself (Prov. 31:22)

    D. Spend time in evaluation (James 1:5; Ps. 90:12).
- "So teach us to number our days, that we may apply our hearts unto wisdom (Ps. 90:12)." Ask God to help you make the most significant use of each day you are given.
    1. Make notes of your evaluation.
    2. Ask God for wisdom (James 1:5).
    3. Evaluate your work areas, such as your kitchen, office, etc.
    4. Seek ways to streamline your work, storage, routines, etc.
    5. Time your duties.
    6. Identify areas in your schedule where you are wasting time.
    7. Make the necessary changes.

E. Write down Biblical goals according to your evaluation, in order to implement the necessary changes.

F. Schedule your days, weeks, months, etc., according to your goals and priorities (I Cor. 14:40).
1. Use a planner to schedule your responsibilities.
2. Write down things you need to do as you think of them.
3. Look at your next day's schedule in the evening.
4. Plan Monday's schedule on Sunday as you think of things to do.
5. Plan the rest of Monday's responsibilities early in the day and as you think of them.
6. Fill in the rest of the week, the months, and the year as events are scheduled.
- ✦ Hint - Keep a pen and a pad of paper in your bathroom and beside your bed. If you think of something while you are doing your hair, putting on your make up, etc., or after going to bed, write it down.

G. Establish good habits.

Develop a routine (for work). The more work you're able to fit into a daily routine, the better. Those things you do everyday (spending time with the Lord, getting dressed, exercising, making coffee), watering the lawn, unloading the dishwasher, making the bed . . . tidying up, fixing breakfast, lunch, and dinner, running errands, etc., take less time when they are part of a routine. Your goal is to be able to say, 'This is when I always walk . . . tidy up. . . .' Then you'll be able to glide effortlessly from one task to the next. Also, because you're used to a routine, you'll have fewer decisions to make, less thinking to do, and less indecision to battle. You'll perform many tasks by rote, leaving your mind free to pray, dream, and plan. Knowing what's coming can also generate an eager and energetic expectation about the next task.[45]

H. In order to shape up my schedule I will _____
_____

II. "Shape Up" your spending.

A. Group your shopping trips to save time and money.

B. Organize your shopping.
- ✦ Hint - Organize your food shopping with lists on envelopes or in plastic folders, in which you can put your coupons.

✦ On my computer I made a shopping list of the stores where I normally shop. I listed the items that I usually purchase at each store, and left space for items which I may need to add to that list. It reminds me of items that I need when making my shopping list. I print several copies at a time and put some in my planner and in my kitchen.
- ✦ Hint - Organize clothes shopping with lists (sizes, fabric swatches, etc.)

- Hint - Organize gift shopping lists ("likes," collections, sizes, etc.)
- Hint - Use your personalized address labels on all rebate forms. Carry some in your wallet and in your coupon box.
- Hint - When items are on sale that you know you will use, buy several extra. Try to get in a cycle of paying less than full price for most items.
- Hint - When running water in the kitchen to get hot water for dishes, put it in a jar to water house plants, or take the time to clean your sink.
- Hint - In warm weather, shut the blinds or shades to keep the heat out of the house. To keep heat in your house in cold weather, open the blinds when the sun is shining and close them when it is cloudy.
- Hint - When clothing (appropriate fabric, probably cotton or a blend) is no longer wearable, tear it into appropriate size "rags". Use them for cleaning instead of paper towels. Toss them when the task is completed. It will cut down on having to purchase paper towels.

C. Limit your spending to fit within your budget.
- The word *budget* means "a plan for coordinating income and expenses."[46]
- "Budget: telling your money where to go instead of wondering where it went."[47]
   1. Make a realistic budget.
       a. Successful budgeting will improve not only your finances, but your outlook on life as well.
       b. Many budgets are wrecked by hidden expenses that are not accounted for.
       c. If you want your budget to work, you need to set aside time on a regular basis to revise and update it.[48]
- Suggested Reading: *"The World's Easiest Guide" to Finances*, by Larry Burkett, published by Northfield Publishing in Chicago, IL., 2000.
   2. Spend within your budget.
   3. Discipline yourself to save.
   4. Use foresight, patience, and improvision.
- Hint - to make inexpensive funnels, cut off the tops of a two-liter soda bottle and a milk jug. (Be sure to include the handle of the milk jug.) These are good for camping, because you can throw them away when you're finished with them. They are also very helpful in the kitchen, especially the milk jug funnel, because you can make its handle the funnel handle.
   5. Pray for God's provision and wisdom in your spending.
   6. Exercise restraint.

D. In order to shape up my finances I will _____

III. "Shape Up" your surroundings.
- Organizing your home makes it more attractive.

A. Organize your food preparation. (See "Menu Planning")
- ✦ Hint - Set your breakfast table in the evening.

B. Organize your cleaning.
- ✦ Hint - After washing your dishes, clean out one shelf in your cabinets or your refrigerator.
- ✦ Hint - Keep baskets at the top and bottom of the stairs or in the front and back of the house to save steps and time.
- ✦ Hint - Put wide "rubber bands" from broccoli bunches on the ends of your broom, mop, etc. This will prevent them from slipping down off the broom rack.

C. Organize your clutter. (See "Eliminate the 'Clutter'")
- ✦ Hint - Put away some accessories for a few months; they will seem new when you bring them out again. You may even decide that you don't need them!
- ✦ Hint - Flatten cardboard boxes (cereals, crackers, etc.), to compact the trash.
- ✦ Hint - Establish a filing system now, even if you have to use cardboard boxes.
- ✦ Hint - Use shoe boxes in your dresser drawers to organize your socks, etc.

D. Organize your children (Prov. 20:11). (See "Teaching Children. . . .")
  1. Teach them to be responsible for their *actions*.
  2. Teach them to be responsible for their *things*.
     Homework
     Lunch
     Clutter
     Room
     Time
     Money
  3. Teach them to be responsible for their *testimony*.
  4. Teach them to be responsible for the completion of their *work assignments*.
  5. Teach them to be responsible for their *laundry*.
  6. Make them fulfill *weekly responsibilities* with written instructions.

✦ The key word is *responsibility*! A diligent homemaker accepts personal responsibility! You must teach your children to also become responsible. They cannot become successful adults without learning that important character quality. Even if they do *not* become responsible, they will be held accountable for their actions and punished accordingly. It is better for them to experience the consequences of irresponsibility when they are young, when the consequences are normally less devastating.

E. Organize your storage.
  1. Files
  2. Seasonal Items
  3. Gifts
  4. Clothing

F. Organize an address file. (See "Eliminate the 'Clutter'")

G. Organize your gift shopping.
- ✦ Hint - I made up a gift inventory sheet for each family for which I purchase gifts. I have a column for each person's name, the gift (Christmas or birthday), the value of the gift, the price I paid, and a column to check off when it is wrapped and given. It helps me keep track of what I have purchased and what I still need to purchase. I shop all year long as I watch for clearance sales. Most of the time I save fifty, even seventy-five percent of the original price.

H. Organize your travel.
   1. Make up a sheet on the computer which lists the following categories.
      General items to pack
      Personal items to pack
      Things to be done before leaving, such as "Stop the newspaper"
      Projects to take on the trip (reading, etc.)
      Phone numbers for immediate family members, employer, doctor, bank, dentist, etc.
      Things to do or "deliver" on the trip
      Finances: bills to pay, cash, etc.
      Food, drinks, hand sanitizer, napkins, etc.
      Things to do when you return
   2. As you think of additional things, add them to your list.
   3. Check off each item as it is packed or completed.
   4. Take your list with you to help you accomplish your goals and to return home with all your necessary items.
   5. Run off a new copy each time you begin to plan for a trip.
- ✦ Hint - Carry baby wipes in your car to remove food spots from clothes.
- ✦ Hint - Store plastic bags in your suitcases. You won't have to hunt for bags while packing. Use them to pack your shoes in, to pack clothes in (to cut down on wrinkles), and to store soiled laundry.
- ✦ Hint - Store hand towels under each seat in your vehicle. Use them as lap covers when you decide to eat in your car.

I. Beautify your home. Be creative!
   1. Pray about it (Phil. 4:6).
- ✦ We had a kitchen, dining room and living room which were all too small for our needs. Grandchildren were being added to the family! The rooms were too small to entertain groups from the church. Also, the kitchen did not have a window, so it lacked good lighting. I read an article which suggested removing a wall when a room does not have enough light. There was an opening in the wall between the living room and dining room. We looked at the blueprint for our house and learned that the wall we wanted to partially remove was not a support wall. We more than doubled the opening by removing more of the existing wall. What a difference! The rooms are much more useable, and the kitchen is much brighter.

- Several years later we began an addition to our house. We had prayed about it for several years. The Lord guided us in the layout and gave us the ideas we needed. We did not have a blueprint drawn up, but God helped us through the process in amazing ways. We drew our own layouts on graph paper, probably using at least twenty-five different layouts! The layout we have is just right for our needs, and it in no way looks like an "add-on." We have enjoyed it so much. The Lord has allowed us to entertain large groups, including our family and our church members. It is a two-story addition with a large room (which has four nice windows) in the lower level. When I am preparing for a large group, I can work a little at a time and leave it until I have time to do more. We had originally wanted the larger room on the main level. One night I was lying awake thinking about the addition. The Lord gave me the idea of putting the larger room on the lower level. What a blessing that idea has been! Ask the Lord to help you build, decorate, and arrange your home.

    2. Clean and organize a room.
- These are the first two ways to improve the beauty of a room. They are also the least expensive ways to improve its attractiveness.

    3 Analyze your existing rooms.
- See if the furniture or accessories in one room might "go better" in a different room.

    4. Rearrange existing rooms.
- The least expensive way to redecorate a room is to rearrange the furniture in the room. Measure the room and all the furniture. Lay out your arrangement on graph paper in pencil. Indicate where the doors and windows are so you know exactly where the furniture will fit. This helps you know if your ideas will work, without wasting time and energy. It might make your husband more receptive to the idea of rearranging the room, if you can show him that the new arrangement will be workable, instead of redoing it several times.
- Hint - A straight pin holds up to ten pounds, but it leaves a very small hole in a wall. Gently pound it into the wall at a downward angle.

    5. Use what you already have.
- When we were redecorating the opening between the living room and dining room, we wanted to make it look more attractive. We had a porch post that had been removed because it had started to rot on the bottom. I couldn't bear to throw it away, so we stored it in our garage. My husband cut off the bottom of the post, split it, removed all the old paint, and installed one half of it on each side of the opening. I then painted it. It looks great and did not cost us anything, except for labor!

    6. Look in magazines and newspapers for ideas.

    7. Notice decorating ideas in other peoples' homes.
- When planning our addition, we drove around to different neighborhoods to get ideas about the size and number of windows that were appealing, structural ideas, etc. That was a great help.

    8. Paint a room, which is the second least expensive way to redecorate a room.

J. Streamline your activities.
1. Handle papers only once.
2. Do not iron only one item.
3. Do all of your weekly shopping in one trip, if possible.
4. Memorize Scripture while you are drying and curling your hair, washing dishes, ironing, etc.

K. In order to shape up my surroundings I will _____
_____

Remember, efficient management at home demands godly priorities and diligent planning. Have you accepted your God-given role as a help meet, a home maker? Do you need to "shape up" in the area of diligence? The difference between diligence and slothfulness is attitude and character, not talent.

Do you need to adjust your priorities and goals according to Scripture? Spend some time evaluating your time schedule. Schedule as much as you can, according to Biblical priorities. Correct, careful planning brings freedom, not bondage.

Do you need to "shape up" your spending? Establish a budget, with the help of your husband. Limit your spending within your budget, and be content with what you have (Heb. 13:5). I told some of my grandchildren that a penny doesn't look very important. However, if they want to buy something for $1.00, and they only have ninety-nine cents, that one little penny will look *very* important!

Do you need to "shape up" your surroundings? Get clutter under control. Spend some time praying, dreaming, and planning how to make your home more attractive. Be creative with what you have! When God created the world, it was in perfect order, and it was beautiful!

Pick your most basic need and begin to make the necessary changes. Believe that efficient management at home demands godly priorities and diligent planning. "Every wise woman buildeth her house, but the foolish plucketh it down with her hands (Proverbs 14:1)."

Eliminate the "Clutter"

C/*lutter* is defined as "crowded confusion."[49] As a verb, it means "to fill with scattered things that impede movement or reduce efficiency."[50] Clutter in the home not only reduces efficiency, but it also wastes money. Clutter in the home results in clutter in the mind. "Clutter wearies the spirit and fights against serenity."[51] Is your house in order, or is it a "visual aid" for the word *clutter*?

God created everything with purpose and order. Everything He created remained that way until man sinned. To be a successful homemaker, you must purpose to have order in your home. *Putting* things in order requires planning and time, and *keeping* it in order requires discipline, time, and cooperation. However, it actually saves time! How many times have you wasted a lot of time searching for a certain item? How many times have you declared, "I *know* I put it right here!" How many times have you cleaned out a room, a drawer or whatever, and found something you had been trying to find for a long time?

Purpose to get your home in order, which will save you time and frustration. Set the example for your children, because God said, "Let everything be done decently and in order (I Corinthians 14:40)."

I. Get apple boxes with lids from supermarkets, or purchase Rubbermaid type containers or cardboard storage boxes with lids.

    A. Have a "throw away" box.

    B. Have a "something else" box.
◆ This "something else" box will keep you from wandering into other parts of your house and getting sidetracked.

    C. Have a "storage" box.
        1. Use this box to store items from the kitchen.
            a. Duplicate items
            b. Items you no longer want
            c. Items you are not using
            d. Items that "might come in handy some day"
        2. Put this box in an inconvenient place.
◆ "If something is so important to you that you'd risk your life to retrieve it from this box, then it belongs in your kitchen. If this box sits on the shelf for a few months, then these items should be given away to someone who needs them."
        3. Use other boxes for the following:
            a. Seasonal items
            b. Seasonal clothing

          c. Mementos

    D. Have a "give-away" or "sell" box.

II. Ask yourself these questions when "uncluttering."

    A. "Do I really need this?" Does it have sentimental or functional value to me?

    B. "How long has it been since I used this?"

    C. "Do I really need so many?" Do you have duplicate items?

    D. "What would be the worst thing that could happen if I got rid of this?"

III. Determine how much time to spend at one setting.

    A. Work for fifteen minutes each day.

    B. Work one to two hours at a time.

    C. Divide jobs into segments, such as two shelves of a closet per day.

IV. Work in a systematic order.

    A. Begin in the kitchen.

    B. Work clockwise around the house.

    C. Clean out and put things in order all the way around your house: each closet, each shelf, and each drawer.

V. Organize the kitchen.

    A. Evaluate your kitchen to decide where best to store items to save time and space.

    B. Store things used twice a year or less.

    C. Use drawer dividers.
        1. Use plastic baskets for dinnerware and kitchen utensils.
        2. Use foil or plastic wrap boxes (with the metal strips removed) for dividers in your drawers for pens, pencils, etc.

    D. Organize items stored in the refrigerator.
        1. Use plastic containers for cheese and lunch meats.

2. Use a large square container that sits on the bottom shelf and slides out to store bottles and jars.

E. Keep a container in the freezer for leftover meat, vegetables, gravies, etc., as a soup base.

F. Store paper napkins and potholders near the microwave to cover and hold dishes.

G. Organize an "Address File" in a three by five or four by six box and keep it near your phone.
   1. Write in pencil, which allows you to make changes.
   2. Write the name (last name, first name) and phone number on the top line of each card.
   3. Write the address on the next lines.
   4. Add birthday and anniversary information to the card, if you desire.
   5. Add, change, or throw away cards as the information changes.
   6. Keep a pencil or pen in the box.

H. After washing your dishes, do some "mini" cleaning to keep your kitchen clean.
   1. Clean one shelf or drawer in your refrigerator/freezer.
   2. Clean one shelf in a cabinet.
   3. Work in an organized manner, working around the room, up and down, etc.

I. Organize a filing system.
   1. Organize your personal files by category, adding categories as necessary.
       Auto records
       Credit card records
       Home records
       Income tax records
       Insurance records
       Loan records
       Medical records
       Message notes
       Mortgage papers (original documents and all payments)
       Personal Bible studies
       Personal records (birth certificates, passports, Social Security, etc.)
       School records
       Warranties
   2. Have separate file folders within each category.
   3. Have a file folder for illustrations, ideas for future messages, etc.
   4. Have a file folder for ideas for decorating.
   5. Have a file folder for recipes you want to try.
   6. Have a file folder on organization.
   7. Have a separate filing area for church/ministry filing.

Ideas for "Eliminating the 'Clutter'" are from Aletha Davis, other sources, or are original with the author.

Meal Planning

The virtuous woman ". . . is like the merchants' ships; she bringeth her food from afar. She riseth also while it is yet night and giveth meat to her household and a portion to her maidens (Proverbs 31:14-15)." The diligent homemaker strives to follow her example and obey the admonition, "Let all things be done decently and in order (I Corinthians 14:40)."

I. Write down your family's "likes" for dinner.

II. Divide meals into meat categories.

III. Write down all the meals that fit into each meat category.

    A. Categorize the meals.
        1. Chicken: roasted, fried, baked, soup, chicken and rice, chicken and broccoli, fajitas, casseroles, etc.
        2. Ground beef: hamburgers, chili, tacos, spaghetti, pizza, sloppy joes, lasagne, casseroles, etc.
        3. Pork: roast, BBQ sandwiches, sweet and sour pork, casseroles, etc.
        4. Beef: roast, stew, sandwiches, soup, casseroles, etc.
        5. Fish: grilled, baked, tuna sandwiches, casseroles, etc.
        6. Turkey: (categories similar to chicken)
        7. Ham: baked, casseroles, sandwiches, breakfast meals, etc.
        8. Meatless meals

    B. List all the ingredients needed to make each recipe.

IV. Choose a method to organize your meals.

    A. Make a monthly calendar.
        1. Write down in each square the meal you want to prepare for dinner.
        2. Leave a few blanks for leftovers and new recipes to try.
        3. Do one or two weeks, if you cannot plan a month of dinners.

    B. Make up a two-month schedule and rotate all year long.

    C. Make your menu schedule seasonally.

    D. Make a list of ten to fifteen meals.

        1. Store all the ingredients in your cabinets.
        2. Choose one of the meals on your list according to your day.

    E. Make a list of twenty to thirty menus on three by five cards and rotate them.

    F. Buy the weekly specials and plan your menus from them.

V. Organize your meal preparation.

    A. Plan your menu and grocery list at the same time.

    B. Plan meals so you will have leftovers for another meal, such as a roast, from which you can have stew, sandwiches, etc.

    C. Freeze leftovers.
        1. Mark and date the containers put into the freezer.
        2. Keep one container in the freezer for leftover meat, vegetables, gravies, etc. Keep adding to it and use it as a vegetable soup base with leftover meat. Put the leftovers in a pan and cover them with water; cover with a lid. Simmer for two to three hours. Let it cool. Pour the broth through a strainer. Discard any bones. Either discard other solids or blend them with the liquids. Freeze the base in one-cup portions, marked with the name and the date. Use for soup stocks or a gravy base.
        3. Cover a turkey carcase with water. (You may need to break the breast bone into several pieces.) Add one-fourth of an onion, one to two stalks of celery, and one to two carrots. Simmer for several hours. Let it cool. Pour the broth through a strainer. Remove the meat from the bones. Discard the vegetables and the bones. Freeze the broth and meat scraps in one-cup portions for soup stock or a gravy base.

- Mark the containers with the name and date.
- The small plastic margarine containers are excellent for freezing food. They hold one-cup portions, and they have lids. Also, it is easy to remove the food from the containers.

    D. Post your grocery list, so family members who use up an item can write it on the grocery list.

    E. Limit sweets for growing children!

    F. Make meals attractive and well-balanced.

    G. Eat leisurely and build good relationships.

    H. Store leftover food in pint and quart glass jars in the refrigerator.
        1. You can see what is in the jar.

2. You can conserve refrigerator space on the shelves.
3. You can see the amount of food available: ½ cup, 1 cup, or 2 cups, etc.

I. Bring all the ingredients from your freezer which are necessary for your meal, and put them into your refrigerator freezer to save "getting ready" time.

J. Keep your menu plans in the kitchen to remind you in the morning what you have planned.

K. Fix what you can after breakfast.

L. Do your baking after breakfast.

M. Budget your money for special times to "eat out."

Ideas for "Meal Planning" are from Aletha Davis, other sources, or are original with the author.

Helps for Laundry Efficiency

1. Place a laundry box or basket in each child's closet. (Hopefully, all the dirty laundry will end up in the basket!)

2. Place marked boxes or baskets in the laundry area for each load of laundry, such as:
    - white (normal wash cycle)
    - white (permanent press wash cycle)
    - light-colored (normal wash cycle)
    - light-colored (permanent press wash cycle)
    - dark (normal wash cycle)
    - dark (permanent press wash cycle)
    - items to hand wash
    - a basket for towels, if they are not washed daily

3. Instruct your children to empty their baskets on wash days, such as Monday, Wednesday, and Friday. (If they do not empty their basket, their clothes will not be washed!)

4. Place written instructions for operating the washer and dryer above each appliance.

5. Have detergents, bleach, a bottle of bleach diluted with water, stain remover, Woolite, hair spray (for removal of ink), fabric softener, etc., available. Use an old tooth brush to scrub stubborn spots from clothing after the spot has been treated with stain remover. Have a cloth available for wiping up spills! <u>Be sure the bottle of diluted bleach is clearly marked!</u>

6. Save small pieces of hand soap in a container to remove stains from clothing. Moisten the area where the fabric is stained or spray it with a diluted Simple Green solution. Rub the stain with hand soap; then rub the stain until it is gone. Put the item into the load of laundry. Most stains will respond to this treatment.

7. Hang a rod (with hangers) for permanent press laundry. Put dried, permanent press clothes on hangers as you remove them from the dryer and hang them on the rod.

8. Instruct those who wash the laundry to fold it after it has been washed and dried. Separate it into piles for each family member. Have a permanent place for each family member's pile of clean laundry.

9. Have your children put away their own laundry.

10. Store a water bottle with a "pop-top" lid near your ironing board. Keep it filled with water in order to easily refill your iron. If the bottle falls on the floor, it will not break or spill.

These ideas can help lessen the mother's "load," help the children learn how to do laundry, and teach the children to be more responsible.

Teaching Responsibility and its Benefits to Children

NAME_____WEEK_____

Responsibilities to be completed	S	M	T	W	Th	F	S	B
Totals								

ALLOWANCE POTENTIAL_____ALLOWANCE EARNED_____

Suggested Guidelines:
1. Write the responsibilities for the child on the chart.
2. Be sure the responsibilities are within your child's capability. Put basic responsibilities, such as "Get out of bed," "Brush your teeth," etc., on the chart. Help your child develop good habits.
3. Be sure the responsibilities are clearly understood by your child.
4. Instruct older children to mark the charts themselves; younger children will need help.
5. Give your child a bonus if he/she does an assigned responsibility every day of the week.
    a. Your child could actually earn <u>more</u> than his potential allowance.
    b. Your child can learn to establish good habits, which reap benefits.
6. Determine the allowance earned by dividing the number of responsibilities actually fulfilled by the number of responsibilities assigned.
7. Award daily, weekly, and monthly rewards:
    a. Daily = mark on the chart
    b. Weekly = allowance
    c. Monthly = have a friend overnight if your child earns three fourths of his/her potential allowance for four weeks in a row.
8. Teach your child to tithe from his/her allowance.
9. Make the charts on your computer. Print or copy them.

Chapter Five

The Help Meet's Prudent Words - "As Choice Silver"

- ✦ Scripture: Proverbs 31:26; 19:14; I Samuel 25; Judges 14-16
- ✦ Principle: A wife must be prudent in order to be a godly help meet.
- ✦ Proverbs 22:3: "A prudent man foreseeth the evil, and hideth himself: but the simple pass on, and are punished."

In order for a wife to do good for her husband all the days of her life, she must possess the quality of prudence. *Prudence* is the process of thinking through matters, which results in wise dealings and use of good practical common sense.[52] According to God's Word, this prudence is from the Lord. "Houses and riches are the inheritance of fathers: and a prudent wife is from the LORD (Proverbs 19:14)." Rich indeed is the man who is blessed with a prudent wife!

To obtain prudence, a wife must know the Lord, possess a humble spirit, study God's Word, and conform her life to It. She then will be equipped to foresee harmful situations and avoid them. She will also learn when to speak, how to speak, and to refrain from speaking in given situations. She will choose her words carefully and with purpose, speaking with wisdom and kindness. Many harmful consequences will be averted for her and her family. A prudent wife will be of great worth to her husband–even more valuable than earthly riches (Proverbs 31:10). *She will do good for her husband!*

I. What is the definition of *prudence*?
II. How is prudence obtained?
III. What are the characteristics of the prudent woman?
IV. How will the prudent woman be rewarded?
V. Who was a Bible example of prudence? Abigail
VI. What is the definition of *simplicity*?
VII. What are the characteristics of the simple woman?
VIII. What are the consequences of the simple woman's refusal of correction?
IX. Who was a Bible example of simplicity? Samson
X. How does a prudent woman compare with a simple woman?
XI. How does a prudent wife affect her husband for good?

I. What is the definition of *prudence*?

A. The Hebrew word *sekel* has several meanings.
   1. It ". . . relates to an intelligent knowledge of the reason."[53] (Prov. 19:14)
   2. "There is the process of thinking through a complex arrangement of thoughts, resulting in a wise thinking, and use of good practical common sense."[54]
   3. It is "to have insight or comprehension . . . conforming one's life to the character of God."[55] (Prov. 1:3)
   4. It means "acting circumspectly or prudently."[56]
      a. The prudent one determines to speak correctly (Ps. 141:3).
      b. The prudent will be silent during evil times (Amos 5:13).
      c. The fool *appears* wise when he is silent (Prov. 17:28).

B. The Hebrew word *orma* means the following:[57]
   1. Positively it means prudent "behavior" (Prov. 1:4).
   2. Negatively it means presumptuous "guile" (Ex. 21:14).

C. Prudence is the ability to reason wisely, speak correctly, and live godly.

D. Application: _____
   _____

II. How is prudence obtained?

A. One must obtain prudence from God.
   1. One must have a relationship with God (Prov. 19:14).
   2. One must have a humble spirit, willing to accept reproof (I Kings 3:3-13; II Chron. 2:12; Prov. 15:5).
   3. One must study God's Word (Ps. 19:7; Prov. 1:4-7; 18:15).
   4. One must apply God's Word (Prov. 1:4-7; James 1:25).

B. Therefore, a wife who possesses prudence is from the Lord (Prov. 19:14).

C. Application: _____
   _____

III. What are the characteristics of the prudent woman?

A. She is humble, willing to accept reproof (Prov. 15:5).

B. She therefore becomes wise, because she has accepted reproof (Prov. 29:15).
   1. She guards her lifestyle by being cautious (Prov. 14:15; 31:27).
   2. She covers shame with loving kindness (Prov. 12:16; I Pet. 4:8).
   3. She speaks correctly and at the right time (Prov. 12:23; 17:27; Amos 5:13; James 1:19).
      a. She withholds information that must be kept private (Prov. 12:23).

        b. She speaks sparingly (Prov. 10:19; 17:27; James 1:19).
    4. She recognizes and avoids evil (Prov. 22:3; 27:12).
    5. She gives of herself for the benefit of others (Prov. 9:1-5).
        a. She cuts down trees to build her house; she does not worship them.
        b. She kills animals for meat; she does not worship them.

C. Application: _____
   _____

IV. How will the prudent woman be rewarded?

A. She will be given knowledge (Prov. 14:18; 18:15).

B. She will be preserved from evil (Prov. 14:3; 22:3; 27:12).

C. She will be spared embarrassment (Prov. 12:16).

D. She will be honored (Prov. 31:28-29).

E. Application: _____
   _____

V. Who was a Bible example of prudence? Abigail (I Samuel 25:3-41)

A. Abigail was godly in character.
    1. She was beautiful, but she was not vain (v. 3).
    2. She was of good understanding (v. 3; Job 28:28; Prov. 9:10; 19:14).
    3. She was humble (vv. 24, 41).
    4. She was obedient to God's will (v. 32).
    5. She had spiritual discernment (knowledge) (vv. 28-31).

B. Nabal was ungodly in character.
    1. He was rich (v. 2), but he was very selfish (vv. 11, 36).
    2. He was cruel (v. 3).
    3. He was easily angered (vv. 10-11).
    4. He was proud (v. 11).
    5. He was unapproachable (v. 17).

✦ The earth protests when a *nabal* grows rich; such a one becomes arrogant and overbearing (Prov. 30:22). The boorishness, a reflection of refusal to listen to reason or to God (at the moment) is seen in Nabal of whom his wife Abigail said, '. . . he is such a son of Belial that no one can speak to him' (I Sam 25:17). He is an *n'bala*, because he rejects the fear of the Lord who could have given him some wisdom.[58] (*sic.*)

    6. He was foolish (v. 25).
    7. He was a son of Belial (v. 17).

C. Abigail reasoned wisely (vv. 15-37).

✦ *Wisdom* (*hokmah*) ". . . is the knowledge and ability to make the right choices at the opportune time. The consistency of making the right choice is an indication of maturity and development. The prerequisite for 'wisdom' is the fear of the Lord. . . ."[59]

1. She analyzed the situation (vv. 18-19, 30-31).
   a. She knew David's men deserved to be fed (vv. 15-16).
   b. She prepared the necessary food (v. 18).
   c. She believed the situation required immediate action and wisdom (vv. 18-31).

A woman must approach her husband or other authorities carefully, with humility and wisdom.

2. She foresaw the potential evil (vv. 28-32).
   a. She saw evil was intended against her husband (v. 17).
   b. She foresaw a tarnished reputation for David (vv. 30-31).
   c. She foresaw a guilty conscience for David (v. 31).

D. Abigail acted wisely to remedy the situation (vv. 18-37; Prov. 16:14).
   1. She took the necessary food to David (vv. 18, 27).
   2. Her motive was to prevent evil, not to manipulate or rule (Prov. 21:9, 19).

E. Abigail spoke wisely to those involved (Prov. 31:26).
   1. Husband (vv. 17-19, 36-37)
      a. She did not speak to him when he was unapproachable (vv. 17-19) or drunk (v. 36).
      b. She did tell him what she had done (v. 37).
   2. David (vv. 24-31)
      a. She requested a hearing (v. 24).
      b. She requested that David disregard Nabal's words and actions (v. 25).
      c. She reminded him that God was in control (vv. 26-29).
      d. She gave him the necessary food (v. 27).
      e. She reminded him that God had a plan for his life (v. 28).
         (1) David's house would be preserved (v. 28).
         (2) David fought for the LORD–not for himself (v. 28).
      f. She reminded him that he had an unblemished testimony (v. 28).
      g. She cautioned David about future grief that would result from exercising vengeance (vv. 30-31).

F. Abigail prevented evil (vv. 31-39).
   1. She prevented future grief for David (vv. 31-39).
      a. David humbly received Abigail's advice in the presence of six hundred soldiers (v. 33).
      b. David did not take vengeance upon Nabal (v. 35).
      c. David let God remove his reproach (v. 39).

                d. David applied that same principle in relation to Saul (I Sam. 26:8-11).
                e. David refused to kill Saul, though Saul tried to murder him (I Sam. 26:11).
  ✦ David was faithful to Saul, despite Saul's jealous, vengeful treatment of him.

  Faithfulness does not guarantee the absence of trials, nor recognition or rewards from man.

            2. She prevented Nabal's death by the hand of David (v. 34).
            3. She prevented death for Nabal's household by the hand of David (v. 34).
  ✦ If David had attacked Nabal, no doubt many men would have died, since David had six hundred soldiers. When left in God's hands, only Nabal died.

      G. God interceded for David.
            1. He smote Nabal (v. 38).
            2. He returned Nabal's evil upon himself (v. 39).

      H. Abigail became David's wife.
            1. She remained humble, willing to serve David's servants (v. 41).
            2. She had one son, Chileab (II Sam. 3:3).

      I. Application: _____
         _____

VI. What is the definition of *simplicity*?

      A. The Hebrew word *peti* has the following meanings.
            1. The adjective form of this word means "foolish, simple."[60]
                  a. "*Peti* generally describes the naive (not deranged) in Proverbs who must be well taught, since an immature person believes anything (Prov. 14:15)."[61]
                  b. The foolish one who refuses to learn will inherit folly, which is the impairment of moral and spiritual values (Prov. 14:18).[62]
            2. "The basic verb form *pata* means to entice, deceive, persuade."[63]
                  a. "The basic verb idea is to 'be open, spacious, wide' and might relate to the immature or simple one who is open to all kinds of enticement, not having developed discriminating judgment as to right and wrong."[64]
                  b. It is the simple young man who is unable to discern the lies of the "strange" woman (Prov. 7:5-21).
                  c. It results in harm, even death (Prov. 7:7; 22:3; 29:17).

      B. The foolish one who refuses correction will remain foolish, be unable to discern evil, be open to enticement, and punished.

C. Application: _____
_____

VII. **What are the characteristics of the simple woman?**

    A. She is proud and refuses to learn from wisdom (Prov. 1:22; 15:5).

    B. She therefore remains foolish, because she has severed herself from the source of wisdom.
        1. She believes anything (Prov. 14:15).
        2. She knows nothing (Prov. 9:13).
        3. She speaks in haste (Eccl. 5:2).
✦ Examples: Eve (Gen. 3:2-3); Jezebel (I Kings 21:7); Zeresh, Haman's wife (Es. 5:14).
✦ Each of these wives had a devastating, evil affect upon her husband.
        4. She does not recognize evil (Prov. 22:3; 27:12).
        5. She takes from others to satisfy herself (Prov. 9:14-17).

    C. Application: _____
_____

VIII. **What are the consequences of the simple woman's refusal of correction?**

    A. She is enticed to sin, such as immorality (Prov. 7:7ff).

    B. She inherits folly (Prov. 14:18).

    C. She is punished (Prov. 22:3; 5:8-13).
✦ If the simple woman totally disregards all correction and instruction and goes into a life of sin, her honor is given to others, her years are given to the cruel, strangers take her wealth, she labors for the cruel, and her body is consumed. She finally concludes, "How have I *hated instruction*, and my heart *despised reproof!* I did not *obey* those who instructed me (5:8-13)." Give careful attention to her devastating testimony before you disregard godly instruction.

    D. Application: _____
_____

IX. Who was a Bible example of simplicity? Samson (Judges 13-16)
✦ Principle: The best preparation for parenthood is to know and obey God's Word.

    A. Samson was characterized by pride.
        1. He rejected instruction or reproof from his parents (14:3).
            a. Samson saw the woman and wanted–yea demanded– that his parents fulfill his demands.
            b. The woman pleased him well–(14:3)–but not for long (14:18-20).

    c. Samson did not pray about this decision, though he prayed when he was thirsty after killing the Philistines (15:18).
  2. He lacked discernment.

 B. Samson was enticed to sin (14:5-8; 16:5-17).
  1. He touched a dead (unclean) animal (13:7; 14:8-9).
  2. He had a relationship with a harlot (16:1).

 C. Samson was deceived.
  1. He believed the lies of those who were using him.
   a. His wife (14:15-17)
   b. His lover, Delilah (16:5-18)
  2. He did not discern their evil ways (14:17; 16:15-17).

 D. Samson spoke foolishly; he told them his secrets (14:17; 16:16-17).

 E. Samson was punished (16:21-24; Prov. 22:3).
  1. He was made blind.
  2. He was bound.
  3. He was humiliated, used as an animal.
  4. He gave the Philistines cause to praise their god Dagon (16:24).

 F. Samson slew many Philistines, at the expense of his own life (16:25-30).

 G. Application: _____
_____

X. How does the prudent woman compare with the simple woman? Proverbs

The Prudent Woman	**The Simple Woman**
1. Accepts reproof - humble	1. Rejects reproof - proud (15:5)
2. Wise	2. Foolish
Guards her lifestyle (14:15)	Believes anything (14:15)
Covers shame lovingly (12:16)	Knows nothing (9:13)
Speaks correctly/at right time (12:23)	Speaks in haste (17:27-28)
Recognizes evil/avoids it (22:3)	Ignorant of evil/punished (22:3)

✦ "A prudent man forseeth the evil, and hideth himself, but the simple pass on and are punished (Prov. 22:3)."

3. Example–Abigail, I Samuel 25	3. Example–Samson, Judges 14-16
Preserved the honor of the future king	Lost his honor
Preserved the lives of her husband and household	Lost his eyesight
	Lost his freedom (imprisoned)

Gained a godly husband   Perished with the ungodly

◆ Because the prudent woman *accepts* reproof, she *becomes* wise and *avoids* evil. Because the simple woman *rejects* reproof, she *lacks* wisdom. *Since she has cut herself off from the only source of knowledge, she is unable to recognize evil and will be punished.*

XI. How does a prudent wife affect her husband for good?

A. She will accept correction and acquire prudence (Prov. 15:5).

B. She will conform her life to God's Word (James 1:25).

C. She will reason wisely, using good common sense (Prov. 12:16; 17:27-28; 22:3).

D. She will speak and refrain from speaking at the correct time (Prov. 12:23; 15:23).

E. She will recognize evil and avoid it (Prov. 22:3).

F. She will guard her lifestyle, desiring to not bring reproach upon her husband (Prov. 12:4).

G. She will cover shame by not revealing private matters to others (Prov. 12:16).

H. Application: _____

Prudence is the ability to reason wisely, speak correctly, and live godly. To possess prudence, you must have a relationship with the Lord. You must keep a humble heart and be willing to accept correction from God's Word and others. The study and application of God's Word must be a daily part of your life. As you make this the pattern of your life, God will give you prudence. You will foresee harmful situations and avoid them, thus sparing yourself, and possibly others, from harm.

However, if you disregard correction, either in God's Word or from those in authority, you will lack prudence and be open to the empty enticements of sin. When you reject God's Word, you sever yourself from the *only* source of wisdom. Consequently, you will be easily deceived and make unwise–even harmful–choices. Your future will hold many regrets. Samson's wife pleased him well–but not for long! Samson loved Delilah, but she sought not *his good*, but *her gain*. He *lost* so much. More importantly, Samson did not wholly accomplish God's purpose for his life. He ultimately became the prisoner of those whom God had ordained that he should conquer (Judges 13:5).

Determine to accept God's instruction and correction, in order to gain prudence, which gives discernment. You will be extremely valuable to your husband, your family, and others whom you influence!

"The tongue of the just is as choice silver: the heart of the wicked is little worth (Prov. 10:20)."

It is difficult to comprehend the truth that the tongue can be more valuable than the heart. However, God's Word declares it to be so. Determine to follow Abigail's example, who preserved–not destroyed–her husband's life. Prudence will help you fulfill your God-given purpose to do good to and for your husband! In order to have God's prudence and protection, you must hear and obey His Word.

◆ Read II Chronicles 18. Answer the following questions.
1. Identify the simple king. _____
2. From whom did he seek advice? _____
3. From whom did he reject counsel? _____
4. Whom did the Lord say would be able to entice him? _____
5. Was he deceived? _____ Why? _____
6. What happened to him? _____
7. Identify the godly king. _____
8. From whom did he seek advice? _____
9. What happened to him? _____
_____

Write a principle about prudence to apply to your life.
_____
_____
_____

Chapter Six

The Help Meet's Meek and Quiet Spirit - "Of Great Price"

- Scripture: Proverbs 12:4; I Peter 3:1-6
- Principle: A help meet's spirit greatly affects her husband, their marriage, and their children.
- Proverbs 12:4: "A virtuous woman is a crown to her husband: but she that maketh ashamed is as rottenness in his bones."

At the Creation of the world God instituted the principle of authority. He ordained the sun to rule the day and the moon to rule the night (Genesis 1:16). Both Adam and Eve were to have dominion over the fish, fowl, every living thing, and the earth (Genesis 1:28). This principle of authority was also part of the marriage relationship in the Garden of Eden. God ordained that the husband should rule his wife (Genesis 3:16).

The woman was fashioned by God from man–for man–to be his helper. "And God saw every thing that he had made, and behold, it was very good (Genesis 1:31)." As a wife acknowledges her role as the helper, with a submissive spirit, she honors her husband and helps unite their relationship. *She will do good for her husband.*

The contentious wife, by her attitude and actions, refuses to submit to God's design for her as the helper. She *is a wife*, but she *is not a help meet.* Her rebellion dishonors and humiliates her husband, becomes a source of irritation, and potentially a source of separation. A wife's refusal to submit is evidence of her contempt for her husband (Esther 1:18). If she is in a position of authority, she has great influence on women under her authority (Esther 1:16-18). Her refusal to submit may even lead to her replacement by another woman (Esther 1:19). *She will do evil to her husband.* "A virtuous woman is a crown to her husband: but she that maketh ashamed is as rottenness in his bones (Proverbs 12:4)."

I. Who is a help meet?
II. What is God's plan for authority in marriage?
III. What is the spirit of a contentious wife?
IV. Who was an example of a contentious wife and a submissive help meet?
V. How do the submissive and contentious wives affect their husbands?

I. Who is a help meet?

    A. A help meet is a wife who was uniquely designed by God to fulfill her husband's needs as his helper, completer, and companion (Gen. 2:18-24).

B. A help meet is a virtuous woman of strength, ability, and moral worth, who is different from the world and highly-treasured (Gen. 2:18-24; Prov. 31:10-29).

C. Application: _____
_____

II. What is God's plan for authority in marriage?

A. The husband is to rule his wife.
  1. God instituted this plan in the Garden (Gen. 3:16).
     a. The man was created first (Gen. 2:7, 18-23).
     b. The woman was deceived, demonstrating her need for a ruler (Gen. 3:1-6, 16-17).

✦ The word *rule* was first used when God commanded the sun to rule ("rule, have dominion, reign") the day. After Eve sinned God told Eve that Adam would rule ("rule, have dominion, reign") over her (Gen. 3:16).

     c. God declared the importance of the principle of authority.
        (1) The word *rule* is used over seventy times in the Old Testament.
        (2) The use of *rule* demonstrates the following:
           the importance of the principle of authority,
           the moral necessity of respect for proper authority,
           the value of it for orderly society and happy living,
           the origin of all authority is God.[65]

The principle of authority was instituted for protection–not for punishment.

✦ God chooses leaders, enables them, sets them apart, and directs others through them (Gen. 3:16; Lev. 8:12; Num. 34:1; 35:1; Deut. 10:8; 18:5; Josh. 1:1; Jud. 6:14-16; 13:15; 14:6; I Sam. 12:6; 16:7; 24:6; I Kings 19:15-16; II Kings 11:30-31; II Ch. 9:8; 11:3; 28:5; 29:11; 36:15; Ezra 1:1; Ps. 78:70-72; 105:17, 26; Rom. 13:1-7; Eph. 5:22-24; 6:1-8; Col. 3:18; Titus 2:5; Heb. 13:7, 17).

  2. God reiterated this plan in the New Testament (Eph. 5:22-24; I Tim. 2:13-14).
     a. The husband is the head of his wife (Eph. 5:23).
        (1) The man was created first by God (I Tim. 2:13).
        (2) The woman was deceived by Satan (I Tim. 2:14).
     b. The *husband*–not the *wife*–pictures Christ as head of the church (Eph. 5:23-25).
        (1) Christ loved the church.
        (2) Christ gave Himself for the church.

B. The wife is to submit to her husband (Eph. 5:22; Col. 3:18; Titus 2:5; I Peter 3:15).
  1. *Submission* means "to arrange yourself in rank under."[66]

✦ *Submit* is a present middle voice imperative verb. It was primarily a military term which meant "to rank under" from two words which mean "to arrange under."[67] In the middle voice it means to "subject one's self." "In non-military use it was a 'voluntary attitude of giving in, cooperating,

assuming responsibility, and carrying a burden.'"[68]
- *Co-operate* means "work jointly toward the same end; comply with a request."
    2. Submission is a voluntary choice of the will.
    3. Submission is a commandment for all wives (I Pet. 3:1).
    4. Submission is an attitude shown by a meek and quiet spirit (I Pet. 3:3-4).
        a. This spirit is a "gentle, mild, meek spirit."[69]
            (1) *Meekness* . . . an "inwrought grace of the soul. . . ,
            (2) exercises of it are first and chiefly towards God . . . ,
            (3) spirit in which we accept His dealing with us as good . . . without disputing or resisting. . . ."[70]
            (4) "Insults and injuries . . . are permitted and employed by Him for the chastening and purifying of His elect."[71]
            (5) Meekness ". . . is the adornment of the Christian profession."[72]
- It must be clearly understood, therefore, that the meekness manifested by the Lord and commended to the believer is the fruit of power. The common assumption is that when a man is meek it is because he cannot help himself; but the Lord was 'meek' because he had the infinite resources of God at His command. Described negatively, meekness is the opposite to self-assertiveness; it is equanimity of spirit that is neither elated nor cast down, simply because it is not occupied with self at all.[73]
        b. This spirit is "quiet, tranquil . . . indicating tranquillity arising from within, causing no disturbance to others."[74]
        c. This spirit is called incorruptible apparel (I Pet. 3:4).
        d. This spirit is most valuable in God's sight (I Pet. 3:4).
- *Great price* (*plutetes*) means "the very end or limit . . . with reference to price, of highest 'cost,' very expensive."[75]
- Man considers a woman's *outward* appearance (her face, hair, bodily shape, jewelry, and clothing, or sadly the lack of it) the basis of her beauty! In *man's* estimation, this determines her value. However, God declares that a woman's inward character, her meek and quiet spirit, determines her value. A meek and quiet spirit is one of the character qualities that makes a virtuous woman's value "far above rubies."
        e. This spirit is hidden–but the evidence of it is greatly detectible.
    5. Submission is based on a trust in God (I Pet. 3:5).
    6. Submission is so important that it is better for a man to remain single than to have a contentious wife (Prov. 21:9, 19).
    7. Submission is so effective that an unsaved husband can be led to the Lord by it (I Pet. 3:1-2).
    8. The submission of Christ is our ultimate example to follow (I Pet. 2:21-23).
- *Example* (*hypogrammos*) literally means ". . . 'an under-writing,' 'to write under, to trace letters' for copying by scholars . . . hence a 'writing copy, an example,' I Pet. 2:21. . . ."[76] Christ left His believers the example of His suffering as a pattern for them to follow. Then, Christ *committed his soul*–He "gave over" His soul to God (I Pet. 2:23).[77]

C. Application: _____
_____

III. **What is the spirit of a contentious wife? Proverbs 12:4; 21:9, 19; 27:15**

   A. *Contentious* means "... to govern, in the whole range of activities of government: legislative, executive, judicial or otherwise."[78]

   B. A contentious wife rules her husband, hindering her husband from ruling as God commanded.

   C. A contentious wife's spirit disgraces her husband (Prov. 12:4)
      1. *Ashamed* means "disgrace."[79]
         a. "To fall into disgrace, normally through failure, either of self or an object of trust."[80]
         b. To bring disgrace upon a parent or spouse:
            (1) Lazy son (Prov. 10:5)
            (2) Wife (Prov. 12:4)
            (3) Foolish servant (Prov. 14:35)
      2. Shame and disgrace result in decay.
         a. The contentious wife's spirit has a decaying effect on her husband's inner spirit.[81]
         b. The contentious wife's spirit destroys–not builds up–her husband's inner spirit (Prov. 19:13).
         c. Internal decay is not usually detected until serious damage has already occurred, which may be difficult to repair.

   D. The contentious wife may drive away her husband (Prov. 27:15).

   E. A contentious wife shames–not sharpens–her husband (Prov. 27:15-17).

   F. Application: _____
   _____

IV. **Who was an example of a contentious wife and a submissive help meet?**

   A. Sarah was a believer (Heb. 11:11).

   B. Abram (her husband) was a believer (Gen. 15:6).

   C. Sarai was an example of a contentious wife (Gen. 16:1-6).
      1. Sarai determined to obtain children by her own efforts (v. 2).
         a. Abram hearkened to Sarai (v. 2).
         b. Sarai gave Hagar to Abram to be his wife (v. 3).
      2. Sarai disobeyed God's Word (Gen. 2:24).
      3. Sarai and Abram reaped disastrous consequences (vv. 2-6).
         a. Reversal of roles

                (1) Sarai became the leader, not the helper, completer, or companion (vv. 2-3).
                (2) Abram became the follower, not the leader (v. 4).
                (3) Hagar became the completer of Abram (v. 4).
            b. Adultery committed by Abram (v. 4).
            c. Conflict
                (1) Sarai and Hagar (v. 4)
                (2) Sarai and Abram (vv. 5-6)
            d. Conflict between Abram's two sons
        4. Sarai did evil to Abram by devising and demanding a plan (Gen. 16:2) to disobey God's plan (Gen. 15:4), in order to get children her own way. This selfish decision produced a son, but it also resulted in division, sorrow, and regret. The results continue even today.

Discontentment, if not dealt with, leads to more sin and possible forfeiture.

        5. Sarai got what she wanted, but then she did not want the son she got!
        6. The result of desires fulfilled in the flesh become undesirable!
            a. David's son, Amnon, loved–then hated–Tamar, after he raped her (II Sam. 13:15).
            b. Judas desired thirty pieces of silver in payment for the betrayal of Jesus (Mt. 26:14-15); later he returned them and hung himself, prior to Jesus' death (Mt. 27:3-5).
            c. Sarai desired a son, but she did not want Ishmael (Gen. 21:3-12).
            d. Israel desired a king (I Sam. 8:6), but later they were under a burden because of their king (I Kings 12:4).
            e. Samson's wife pleased him well–but not for long (Jud. 14:3, 17).
        7. Sin sometimes changes relationships in ways that cannot be changed or are very difficult to restore. Examples:
            Abram, Sarai and Hagar's relationships (Gen. 16:1-16)
            King Saul and the prophet Samuel (I Sam. 15:1-35)

    D. Sarah was an example of a submissive help meet.
        1. Sarah followed Abram's leadership (Gen. 12:5-6; Heb. 11:8).
        2. Sarah called Abram lord (Gen. 18:12; I Pet. 3:6).
        3. Sarah adorned herself with a meek and quiet spirit (I Pet. 3:4-6).
        4. Sarah, an example of a woman of faith (Heb. 11:11), trusted in the Lord (I Pet. 3:5-6).
        5. Sarah is our role model to follow (I Pet. 3:6).

    E. Application: _____
    _____

V. How do the submissive and contentious wives affect their husbands?

Submissive Wife - Does Good (commended)	Contentious Wife - Does Evil (condemned)
A. Helps her husband (Gen. 2:18)	A. Hinders her husband
B. Completes her husband (Gen. 2:20-24) Her goal is to fulfill his needs.	B. Competes with her husband Her goal is to win!
C. Honors her husband (Prov. 12:4; 31:23; Es. 1:20)	C. Humiliates her husband (Prov. 12:4; Es.1:13-20)
D. Unites their marriage (Companion, Gen. 2:18)	D. Divides their marriage (Irritation, Prov. 19:13; 21:9, 19; 25:24; 27:15)
E. Illustrated by Sarah (I Pet. 3:6)	E. Illustrated by Sarai (Gen. 16:1-6)
F. Potential salvation of her husband (I Pet. 3:1)	F. Potential salvation of her husband is not mentioned

G. Application: _____

The principle of authority is part of God's plan for order in Creation. It was instituted as part of the husband and wife relationship in the Garden of Eden. God ordained that the husband should rule his wife and she should submit to him. As a wife submits to her imperfect husband, trusting the results to a Perfect God, she can help her husband and do her part to help unite their marriage. She can help bring order to their home. *She will do good for her husband!*

A contentious wife shames the man who should be her companion and best friend. It is difficult to understand why a wife would want to shame or drive away the one who should be her *closest* friend. *She will do evil to her husband!*

Sarah was an example of a contentious wife. She failed in her faith concerning the promise of a son. She then took over the leadership of her home, which resulted in disaster. She indeed did evil to Abram, and to others, in her determination to "do it her way." Her failure was recorded for all who choose to read her story.

However, in the book of I Peter, she is commended as a wife who *obeyed* her husband, as she trusted in the Lord; she even called Abraham "lord" after her failure in Genesis 16. We are commanded to follow her example of submission to her husband. Also, she is commended in Hebrews eleven as one of the faithful ones. "Through faith also Sara herself received strength to conceive seed, and was delivered of a child when she was past age, because she judged him faithful who had promised (Heb. 11:11)."

Sarah's faith in God must have been strengthened after her failure.
Her faith was recorded for all to observe.

No wife will experience perfection in the area of submission. When you fail, you must confess it to the Lord and to your husband. Then, begin again. You must realize submission is a daily, even hourly choice, done by faith. It is enabled by your trust in your Almighty God.

At your wedding, you promised to love, honor, and obey your husband. Have you been true to your vows? Are you ". . . voluntarily giving in, cooperating, assuming responsibility, and carrying a burden . . ."[82] as a helper to your husband? If you are single and marry later, you will vow to "love, honor, and obey" your husband. *Remember, a help meet's spirit greatly affects her husband, their marriage, and their family.*

If you are married, ask yourself the following questions:
- Do I possess a mild, gentle spirit? _____
- Am I willing to be governed by my husband, even if I do not agree? _____
- Do I teach my children, by personal example, to honor their father? _____
- Do I think my husband is the "greatest"? _____
- Does he know that? _____
- Do I disgrace my husband with my contentious spirit? _____
- Do I nag my husband? _____
- Do I appear to submit, but in reality control my husband? _____
- Do I pray daily for my husband? _____
- Do I need to confess my failure to submit and begin again? _____

Chapter Seven

The Help Meet's Great Influence - "For Good, Not Evil!"

- ◆ Scripture: Proverbs 31:12
- ◆ Principle: A help meet exerts influence on her husband all the days of her life.
- ◆ Proverbs 31:12: "She will do him good and not evil all the days of her life."

A virtuous woman is an unselfish woman of strength, ability, and moral worth, who is different from the world and highly treasured. Her virtue is evidenced by her unselfish service for others. God's Word states that this woman will do good for her husband all the days of her life. This can include the days prior to, during, and after their marriage ends, if she outlives her husband. She is truly a help meet.

Ruth honored Mahlon, contributing to his good, even after she became his widow. She dedicated herself to the care of Naomi for the remainder of her own life (Ruth 1:16-17). She could no longer help Mahlon, but she honored him as she chose to help Naomi, his mother, her mother-in-law.

However, not *every* wife is a help meet. A wife can do evil to her husband because of her ungodly character and selfish choices. In order to "do good" for her husband, both a wife's character and decisions must be godly. These directly or indirectly affect her husband for either good or evil. Eve was innocent in character, but she made a selfish choice. She then influenced Adam to do the same.

Not only do a wife's decisions affect her and her husband, but many decisions will have long-lasting consequences on the lives of others. Eve influenced Adam to disobey the only restriction God had placed upon them. Adam's disobedience plunged the human race into sin, which resulted in a death sentence for all mankind. Sarai's selfish demand upon Abram gave birth to a nation which is still at enmity with her own son's seed. In contrast, the Jews were preserved as a nation as a result of Esther's godly influence on her husband, King Ahasuerus.

A wife, who is an evil influence, fails to fulfill God's purpose for her life. A help meet, who influences her husband for good, glorifies God and fulfills His unique and marvelous purpose for her creation.

I. How can a wife be a good influence on her husband?
II. Who were some wives who influenced their husbands for good?
III. How can a wife be an evil influence on her husband?
IV. Who were some wives who influenced their husbands for evil?
V. What principles can be learned from these wives?

I. How can a wife be a good influence on her husband?

    A. She can be a good influence by accepting her role as a helper.

    B. She can be a good influence through her godly character (Prov. 31:10; 12:4).

    C. She can be a good influence with her words and works (Prov. 31:11-27).

    D. She can be a good influence because of her desires, which govern her decisions.

    E. She can be a good influence, regardless of her husband's character (I Cor. 7:12-14; I Pet. 3:1-2).

    F. Application: _____

II. Who were some wives who influenced their husbands for good?

    A. Abigail was a good influence on Nabal (I Samuel 25).
        1. Abigail's character: virtuous
            a. Good understanding (v. 3)
            b. Diligent in her work (v. 18)
            c. Humble in spirit (vv. 24, 41)
            d. Prudent in actions and words (vv. 18-37)
        2. Nabal's character: ungodly (v. 17)
           (See Chapter Four for further information about Nabal.)
        3. Abigail's desire: She desired to prevent the death of her husband and shame for David.
        4. Abigail's decision (vv. 18-37): She decided to provide the food which David's messengers had requested, in order to protect her husband's life and her future king's honor.
            a. Reasoned wisely (vv. 18-20)
            b. Acted wisely to remedy the danger (vv. 18-20)
            c. Spoke wisely to those involved (vv. 23-33; 36-37)
        5. Abigail's influence (vv. 31-39):
            a. She prevented immediate death for Nabal and their household (v. 34).
            b. She prevented future grief for David (vv. 30-31).

✦ Abigail did what Nabal had refused to do (feed David's men), and she prevented what David had determined to do (kill Nabal's household).

        6. Abigail did good for Nabal. She did not disgrace him while trying to prevent his death because of his stubbornness and selfishness.
        7. Application: _____

B. Esther was a good influence on King Ahasuerus (Esther 2-8).
 1. Esther's character: Virtuous
  a. Virgin (2:3)
  b. Found favor in the sight of all men (2:15)
  c. Obedient to her authority (2:10, 20)
  d. Unselfish (2:15)
 2. Ahasuerus' character: Unbeliever (King of Persia)
 3. Esther's desire: She desired to prevent the annihilation of her nation.
 4. Esther's decision (4:16): She decided to go before her husband, King Ahasuerus, to preserve her nation, even at the cost of her own life.
  a. Disregarded Persian law (4:11)
  b. Disregarded her own personal safety for the sake of others (4:16)
  c. Demeanor of her request
   (1) Fasted (4:16)
   (2) Surrendered the results to God (4:16)
   (3) Deceived not, nor connived as Haman had done

Women whose husbands are in authority must realize they have great influence on their husbands, and on others who observe their lives. (Es. 1:16)

   (4) Adorned herself appropriately as the queen (5:1)
   (5) Requested–not demanded (5:4)
    She presented her request humbly.
    She presented her request wisely–she included Haman (5:5).
    She presented her request patiently–she invited both the king and Haman to two banquets (5:4, 8).
   (6) Reverenced her husband's position, which it rightfully deserved

✦ When King Ahasuerus commanded the former queen Vashti to come before him, she *refused to obey*. Queen Esther approached the king, though she had *not been summoned* to come before him. Esther, not Vashti, reverenced her husband's position and authority.

  d. Results of her decision and demeanor (5:2)
   (1) Esther gained favor in the king's sight as she presented herself correctly and her request humbly.
   (2) God worked in her husband's heart (Prov. 21:1).
   (3) Esther's request was granted (5:5; 7:1).
 5. Esther's influence:
  a. Haman was hung on the gallows he had prepared for Mordecai (9:7-10, 13-14).
  b. Haman's sons were killed, then hung by the Jews (9:7-10, 13-14).
  c. Israel was preserved as a nation (8:11).
  d. King Ahasuerus was spared from a curse (Gen. 12:3).
  e. Israel experienced joy, not sorrow (9:17).
  f. Mordecai was promoted to Haman's position (8:2; 10:2-3).

g. Esther was honored. A book of the Bible, bearing her name, records her story of unselfish courage on behalf of her nation Israel.
 6. Esther did good for Ahasuerus. She saved him from a curse placed on nations which cursed Israel (Gen. 12:3).
 7. Application: _____
 _____

C. The Shunammite Woman was a good influence on her husband (II Kings 4:8-17).
 1. Her character: Godly
    a. Servant's heart (v. 8)
    b. Spiritual awareness (v. 9)
    c. Contented (v. 13)
 2. Her husband's character: He was probably a believer, and though he was old, he provided for his family (vv. 14, 18).
 3. Her desire: She desired to care for Elisha's needs.
 4. Her decision: She decided to enlarge her house to better serve one of God's prophets.
    a. She sought her husband's permission (v. 10).
    b. She requested–not demanded–to help a servant of God.
 5. Her influence:
    a. The needs of Elisha were met as he traveled as a faithful prophet of the Lord (vv. 10-13).
    b. The Shunammite woman and her husband were blessed with a son (vv. 16-17).
 6. The Shunammite Woman did good for her husband. She and her husband were blessed with a son.
 7. Application: _____
 _____

D. Ruth was a good influence on both of her husbands (Ruth 1-4).
 1. Ruth's character: Virtuous (3:11)
    a. Trusted in God (1:16)
    b. Virtuous in man's sight (3:11)
 2. Ruth's husbands' character:
    a. Mahlon: Unknown, but he married a pagan
    b. Boaz: Believer
 3. Ruth's desire: She desired to care for Naomi for the remainder of Naomi's life.
 4. Ruth's decision: She chose to live with and serve Naomi (1:16).
    a. She worked to supply Naomi's needs (2:11).
    b. She submitted to the authority over her (3:5).
 5. Ruth's influence:
    a. Naomi's needs were met.
    b. Boaz was blessed with a virtuous wife (4:10).
    c. Boaz and Ruth were blessed with a son (4:13).

        d. Naomi was blessed with a grandson (4:15).
        e. Ruth was brought into the lineage of Christ (Matt. 1:5).
        f. Ruth was honored. A book of the Bible, which bears her name, records the story of her covenant of faithfulness.
    6. Ruth did good for both of her husbands. Ruth honored Mahlon by maintaining a good testimony as his widow. Boaz was blessed with a virtuous wife.
    7. Application: _____
    _____

III. How can a wife be an evil influence on her husband?
✦ (I Kings 21:1-14) "When, instead of a help meet, a man has an agent for Satan, in the form of an artful, unprincipled, yet beloved wife, fatal effects may be expected."[83]

   A. She can be an evil influence by rejecting her role as a helper.

   B. She can be an evil influence through her ungodly character (Prov. 12:4).

   C. She can be an evil influence with her words and works.

   D. She can be an evil influence because of her desires, which govern her decisions.

   E. She can be a hindrance, rather than a helper.

   F. Application: _____
   _____

IV. Who were some wives who influenced their husbands for evil?

   A. Eve was an evil influence on Adam (Gen. 3).
       1. Eve's character: innocent (Gen. 1:31)
       2. Adam's character: innocent (Gen 1:31)
       3. Eve's desire: Eve desired what God had forbidden (Gen. 2:9, 17).
       4. Eve's decision (v. 6): She chose to eat the fruit, desiring to be like God, knowing good and evil.
           a. She had been created to be Adam's helper for good, not evil.
           b. She had no excuse.
           c. She did not become like God!
       5. Eve's influence:
           a. Adam disobeyed God's commandment, which resulted in death for all mankind (Rom. 5:12; I Cor 15:22).
           b. The woman would have sorrow in the childbearing process (v. 16).
           c. The serpent was cursed (v. 14).
           d. The ground was cursed (v. 17).
           e. Man would have to toil for his food (v.17).

6. Eve did evil to Adam. She influenced Adam to disobey God's only restriction on man. Adam's sin resulted in death for all mankind.
7. Application: _____

B. Sarai was an evil influence on Abram (Gen. 16:1-6).
1. Sarai's character: godly
   a. Example of faith (Heb. 11:11)
   b. Example of submission (I Pet. 3:6)
2. Abram's character: godly (righteous) (Gen. 15:6)
3. Sarai's desire: She desired a child more than she wanted God's will–what God had promised, but not yet given.
4. Sarai's decision: She decided to obtain children by giving her handmaid Hagar to her husband (Gen. 16:1-6).
   a. She was discontent with God's plan and timing (v. 2).
   b. She determined to get a child her way (v. 2).
   c. She demanded that Abram implement her plan (v. 2).
5. Sarai's influence:
   a. There was a reversal of roles.
      (1) Sarai became the leader, not the helper, completer, or companion of Abram.
      (2) Abram became the follower, not the leader, of Sarai.
      (3) Hagar became Abram's completer–not Sarai's handmaid.
   b. Abram committed adultery (v. 4).
   c. Hagar conceived a son (v. 4).
   d. There was conflict between Sarai and Hagar (vv. 4-5).

   Abram then had not just one–but two–unhappy wives!

   e. There was conflict between Sarai and Abram (vv. 5-6).
   f. Sarai did not want the son who had been conceived (16:6).
   g. There was (and is) conflict between the sons conceived.
6. Sarai did evil to Abram. She by-passed God's plan to fulfill her desires her own way, which resulted in sin and sorrow for all involved.

✦ When you seek to fulfill your desires your way, you will be greatly disappointed.
7. Application: _____

C. Lot's wife had an evil influence on her husband (Gen. 19).
1. Her character: unknown
2. Lot's character: righteous–but carnal (II Pet. 2:7-8)
3. Her desire: She desired the pleasantries of Sodom more than the deliverance God had provided.

4. Her decision: She disobeyed the angel's command to not look back (vv. 17,26).
    a. Motivated by materialism (Lk. 17: 31-32)
✦ Lot evidently had that same motivation when Abram allowed him to choose the land he desired (Gen. 13:10-13; 14:12).
    b. Motivated by concern for her family?
5. Her influence:
    a. She died (v. 26).
    b. Lot had no helper to meet his needs (v. 31).
    c. Lot and his daughters committed incest (vv. 30-38).
    d. Lot's two daughters bore sons which produced wicked nations, the Moabites (v. 37) and the Ammonites (v. 38).
6. She did evil to Lot. Because of wrong values, she left her husband without a helper, completer, and companion–open to enticement.
7. Application: _____

D. Job's wife had an evil influence on her husband (Job 1:1-2:10).
    1. Her character: foolish (2:10)
    2. Job's character: godly (1:1, 8)
    3. Her desire: She may have desired to end Job's suffering.
    4. Her advice: "Curse God and die (2:9)."
✦ This is exactly what Satan had said Job would do (2:5). *Curse* (2:9) is the same Hebrew word used in Job 2:5. Job's wife must have thought if Job did not have all the blessings God had provided, his life was not worth living.
    5. Her influence: She did **not influence** Job to sin (2:10).
        a. Job rebuked his wife.
        b. Job recognized that God is always righteous in His decisions.
        c. Job refused to act upon her advice.
        d. Job did not serve God only because of the blessings he received.
        e. Job did not sin with his mouth.
✦ The man who *controls his mouth* is called a perfect man, one who is able to also control his body (James 3:2). The man who has *knowledge* spares his words (Prov. 17:27). It takes a person of godly character to refrain from criticism, especially when others are being critical. The genuineness of Job's godly character was validated by his words (Mt. 12:37).
    6. She did evil to Job.
        a. She encouraged him to sin, exactly as Satan had predicted (2:5, 9).
        b. She was a potential source of disappointment, discouragement, and loneliness.
        c. She tried to avoid God's process of purification in Job's life (23:10).
        d. She was not Job's helper–nor best friend–in his greatest trial.

E. Application: _____

- True friends love at all times, which proves their loyalty (Prov. 17:17).
- True friends do not forsake friends in times of trouble, which proves their loyalty.
  "Thine own friend, and thy father's friend, forsake not . . . (Prov. 27:10)."
- True friends make their friends better, not bitter, which proves their love.
  "Iron sharpeneth iron: so a man sharpeneth the countenance of his friend (Prov. 27:17)."
- True friends demonstrate sacrificial love, which proves their love and loyalty.
  "Greater love hath no man than this, than that a man lay down his life for his friend (John 15:13)."
  ". . . he (Jonathan) loved him (David) as his own soul (I Sam. 20:17). . . ."
  Jonathan knew Saul, his father, was determined to kill his friend David, so Jonathan ate no meat that day (I Sam. 20:34).
- True friends are honest at all times, even in difficult situations, which proves their loyalty. "If I knew evil was determined against you, I would tell you (I Sam. 20:9)."
- True friends lift up their friends when they are down, which proves their love and loyalty.
  "For if they fall, the one will lift up his fellow: but woe to him that is alone when he falleth; for he hath not another to help him up (Eccl. 4:10)."
- Though Job did not fall, he could have used encouragement. However, none of his friends, not even his wife, encouraged him.
- A wife who is loyal doesn't say, "He hurt me, so I'll hurt him."
- A wife who is loyal doesn't say, "He wasted money on something he didn't need, so I'll get something for myself, too!"
- A wife who is loyal doesn't say, "If he can do that to me, I'll do _____ to him."

V. What principles can be learned from these wives?

    A. A wife's character should affect her husband for *good*.

    B. A wife's words and works should affect her husband for *good*.

    C. A wife's desires, which govern her decisions, should have a *good* influence on her husband.
        1. Salvation establishes her moral worth, which is a *good* influence on him.
        2. Obedience to God is a *good* influence on him.
        3. Submission to her husband's leadership does *good* for her husband,
            regardless of his character,
            regardless of his treatment of her,
            regardless of the results.
        4. Acting in kindness, not reacting in anger, has a *good* influence on her husband (Eph. 4:31-32; Prov. 25:15).

    D. A wife's choices should have *beneficial* effects on her husband.

    E. A wife must focus on her husband, not on herself, in order to do good for her husband.

    F. Application: _____

- Abigail desired to prevent death for her husband and a tarnished reputation for David. She decided to appeal to David and give him and his men the food they needed. Lives were saved.
- Esther desired to preserve her nation. She decided to fast and appeal to her husband, even at the cost of her life. Her nation was preserved, and she saved her husband from a curse.
- The Shunnamite woman desired to provide for Elisha's needs. She decided to appeal to her husband to add private living quarters for Elisha. She and her husband were rewarded with a son.
- Ruth desired to make sure her mother-in-law Naomi was cared for the remainder of her life. She decided to leave her land, people, and gods and live in Naomi's land. She made Naomi's people her people and Naomi's God her God. She was blessed with a godly husband and son.
- Eve desired to be wise. She decided to disobey God's Word, and lost her innocence.
- Lot's wife desired "stuff." She decided to look back at Sodom, which cost her her life and Lot his wife.
- Sarai desired a child more than God's will. She decided to give her husband another wife. That wife bore a son whom Sarai never loved.
- Job's wife may have desired to end his suffering. She decided to tell him to "Curse God and die!" She failed to support and encourage her husband in his greatest trial.
- Whom did the wives who had a good influence focus on? _____!
- Whom did the wives who had an evil influence focus on? _____!

Let's review the wives who had a good influence on their husbands.

1. Abigail behaved wisely in spite of her ungodly, unreasonable husband, Nabal. She saved her husband's life. She also helped preserve the godly reputation of David, whom she later married.

2. Queen Esther presented herself correctly and her request humbly to her unbelieving husband, King Ahasuerus. She left the results with God; her husband was saved from a curse, and her nation was spared from annihilation.

3. The Shunammite woman's desire to serve others did not cause her to usurp her husband's authority, nor neglect him. They were blessed with a son.

4. Ruth honored her former husband, Mahlon, even after his death, by sacrificially caring for his mother. Boaz, her second husband, was blessed with a virtuous wife and a son.

Let's review the wives who had a destructive influence on their husbands.

1. Eve influenced Adam to disobey God's only restriction on them. Adam's sin brought death, to himself, and to the entire human race.

2. Sarah influenced Abram to disregard God's plan to bring forth their *promised* son, and an *illegitimate* son was born. The hatred between the seeds of the two sons still exists today.

3. Lot's wife made material goals her priority, but she lost everything, even her life. Lot was left without a helper, completer, and companion to fulfil his needs. Her daughters purposely committed incest with their father. Thus, after the destruction of Sodom and Gomorrah, the progenitors of two more evil nations were fathered by Lot and born to his daughters.

4. Job's wife did not fulfill her role as his helper and companion in a time of trial and great affliction.

Two of the wives, Abigail and Esther, were married to *ungodly* men; yet, each of these wives was a *good* influence on her husband. Eve, Sarai, and Job's wife, who each had a *destructive* influence on her husband, were married to *godly* men. A wife must do good for her husband, despite his character. In contrast, even if a wife has a godly husband, that does not guarantee that she will have a beneficial influence on him. A wife must have godly *character and desires* in order to do good for her husband. A wife must first focus on doing good for her husband, not herself!

Have you failed to be a good influence on your husband? If so, you must ask the Lord and your husband for forgiveness. Claim a Scripture verse to strengthen you when you are again tempted by *evil desires* to make *selfish* choices. You must *choose* to do good–not evil–to and for your husband, each day of your life (Proverbs 31:12).

Chapter Eight

The Help Meet's Captivation - "Loving and Kind"

- ✦ Scripture: Genesis 2:18-25; Proverbs 5:15-21; 31:11; I Corinthians 7:1-5
- ✦ Principle: A help meet must lovingly fulfill her husband's personal, physical needs.
- ✦ Proverbs 5:19: "Let her be as the loving hind and pleasant roe: let her breasts satisfy thee at all times: and be thou ravished always with her love."

Americans live in an Age of Sensuality. There is hardly a commercial product which is not marketed with a sensual focus–even pizza! Never has there been a period in America's history when there was more knowledge, encouragement, and practice of illicit sex and sensuality. Has this helped marriages? No! "The median duration of first marriages that end in divorce is about 6.3 years."[84]

Frigid, unresponsive wives. Unfulfilled husbands. What is the answer? Is it a sensual focus with everything having a sexual undertone and interpretation? No! Christians do not need a sensual focus to create sexual fulfillment in their marriage. The sensual focus says, "Please me! Satisfy me! Give to me!"

However, God's Word teaches that happiness does not come from lusting and taking what one wants. ". . . Lust . . . when it is finished, bringeth forth death (James 1:15)." "Charity (love) . . . seeketh not her own (I Corinthians 13:5). . . ." After serving His disciples by washing their feet, Christ said to them, "If ye know these things, happy are ye if ye do them (John 13:17)." Therefore, fulfillment and satisfaction are the result of knowing and obeying God's principles for marriage, joyfully *giving*, not selfishly *taking*, within the marriage relationship.

Christians must have a selfless, not a sensual focus in their marriage.

God created marriage and the sexual relationship within its boundaries. Some refer to it as the act of marriage, since it is lawful only within marriage. It is God's ordained physical oneness between the husband and his wife. It is the unselfish *giving* of oneself for the *benefit* of the other, the help meet and her husband, each for the other. *As a wife does this, she can do good, not evil, for her husband each day of their marriage.*

I. Who created physical oneness within marriage?
II. Why did God create physical oneness within marriage?
III. What guidelines did God establish for physical oneness?

IV. How should a wife respond to her husband?
V. What might happen if a wife refuses to fulfill her husband's sexual needs?
VI. What are the results of pleasant sexual relations for the husband and wife?

I. Who created physical oneness within marriage?

    A. Physical oneness within marriage was created by God (Gen. 1:28).

    B. Physical oneness within marriage was declared by God to be good (Gen. 1:31).

    C. The desire of the husband and the wife for each other was given by God (Gen. 1:27-28).

    D. Application: _____

II. Why did God create physical oneness within marriage?

    A. God created it to replenish the earth (Gen. 1:27-28).

    B. God created it for pleasure (Prov. 5:15-19).

    C. God created it for the prevention of illicit sex (I Cor. 7:2).

    D. Application: _____

III. What guidelines did God establish for physical oneness?

    A. It is to be fulfilled only within the boundary of marriage between a man and a woman (Gen. 2:24; Prov. 5:17; Heb. 13:4).

✦   Eve became a wife *before* she became *one* physically with her husband.

    B. It is not shameful, but it is private (Gen. 2:25).

    C. It helps prevent fornication when fulfilled legitimately (I Cor. 7:2).

    D. It may be abstained from temporarily, by mutual consent (I Cor. 7:5).

    E. It must be re-established to avoid fornication (I Cor. 7:5).
        1. The word *incontinency* means "want (lack) of self-control."[85]
        2. A refusal to resume the physical relationship robs either the husband or the wife of the pleasure which is due them.

3. A failure to resume the relationship may result in a temptation to be unfaithful.

F. The unlawful use of sexual relations is sinful and will be judged by God (Heb. 13:4).

G. Application: _____

IV. How should a wife respond to her husband?

A. The wife must realize she was created to be her husband's physical completer and companion (Gen. 2:20-24).

B. The wife must learn to love her husband (Titus 2:3-4; Gen. 3:16).

C. The wife must be kind and generous (I Cor. 7:3).
   1. *Benevolence* means "goodwill."[86]
   2. Kindness and generosity are choices–not emotions.

D. The wife must realize her body belongs to her husband (I Cor. 7:4).

E. The wife must determine to captivate her husband (Prov. 5:19).
   1. The wife must be loving (Prov. 5:19).
   2. The husband should be *ravished* or "fully satisfied" by his wife.[87]

F. The wife's brain is sometimes the most important part of her body in the sexual relationship.
   1. She must keep herself physically attractive.
   2. She must not exhaust herself with too many obligations, making herself physically incapable of lovingly giving herself to her husband.
   3. She must determine to keep communication open.
   4. She must determine to be receptive to his desires.

G. Application: _____

V. What might happen if a wife refuses to fulfill her husband's sexual needs?

A. He may choose adultery, pornography, etc.

B. He may feel degraded.

C. He may experience resentment and self-pity.

D. He may become bitter toward his wife.

E. He will become the follower, not the leader.

F. Application: _____

VI. What are the results of pleasant sexual relations for the husband and wife?

✦ A. The husband can safely trust in his wife, needing nothing or no one else (Prov. 31:11). Remember, *safely trust* means "to trust," and ". . . expresses that sense of well-being and security which results from having something or someone in whom to place confidence . . . stressing the feeling of being safe and secure."[88]

B. The husband should be captivated (Prov. 5:19; Song of Solomon 4:9).

C. The husband might praise his wife (Song of Solomon 4:9ff.).

D. The husband and wife will fulfill all three purposes for which God created physical oneness within marriage.

E. The husband and wife will both experience pleasure.

F. The husband and wife will not experience God's judgment for illicit relationships (Heb. 13:4).

G. Application: _____

The wife has the responsibility to unselfishly satisfy and captivate her husband. This is her best defense against the strange woman. (Prov. 7:5-27) *She will do good–not evil–for her husband all the days of their married lives.*

In review, God established physical oneness within marriage, and it is good. However, God judges illegitimate sex. Physical oneness:
- may be fulfilled legitimately only within marriage between a man and a woman.
- was created for procreation, pleasure, and prevention of illicit sex.
- is not shameful, but it is private.
- may be abstained from temporarily, legitimately, only by mutual consent.
- must be re-established to prevent illegitimate sex.

A wife must lovingly accept her role as her husband's physical completer and learn to love him unselfishly. She must choose to respond kindly and generously, knowing her body belongs to her husband–not herself. If not, her unfulfilled husband may become resentful and look for sexual satisfaction elsewhere. This will have devastating effects on her husband, her marriage, herself, their children, and the testimony of God. Her husband must accept responsibility for his actions, but she will have done evil to her husband and their marriage. She must determine to captivate her husband with her love–for God's glory (I Corinthians 10:31)!

> *Remember, sin sometimes changes relationships*
> *in ways that cannot be reversed,*
> *or are very difficult to restore.*

Determine to captivate your husband with your love! Remember that ". . . whatsoever ye do, do all to the glory of God (I Corinthians 10:31)."

Chapter Nine

The Help Meet's Honorable Clothing - "Designed by God"

- Scripture: I Timothy 2:9-10
- Principle: A help meet's clothing must distinguish her as a godly woman because of her professed relationship with the LORD.
- I Timothy 2:9-10: "In like manner also, that women adorn themselves in modest apparel, with shamefacedness and sobriety; not with broided hair, or gold, or pearls, or costly array: But (which becometh women professing godliness) with good works."

As a verb the word *distinguish* means "recognize, show, or treat as different; be an identifying characteristic of." *Distinguish oneself* means "make oneself worthy of respect."

Your clothing sends a distinct message.

It *should* send a message that distinguishes you as *a female–not a male* (Deut. 22:5). It *should* send a message that distinguishes you as *godly–not ungodly* (I Tim. 2:10). It *should* send a message that distinguishes *you* and *others* as *worthy of respect* (*shamefacedness*)–not disrespect (I Tim. 2:9).

As a godly woman, your clothing should not cause men to either indulge in sensual thoughts or fight a mental, spiritual battle with sensual thoughts. In the Civil War the uniform worn by Union soldiers was distinctly different from the Confederate soldier's uniform. A Union soldier would not have dared to wear the Confederate uniform–and remain in the Union camp. It would have caused confusion–maybe even have been interpreted as treason, resulting in arrest–perhaps even death.

If you dress in a sensual way, you have joined the forces of Satan–you are one of his soldiers. You are fighting on the wrong side of the spiritual battle. You cannot fight on the Lord's side by wearing the "uniform" of the world. This causes confusion and is treason against the Lord and His other soldiers. The worst deceit and treason is to wear the uniform of an army to which you do not belong. You will be shooting and possibly wounding soldiers on both sides. It could result in a moral wound–or perhaps even death for you.

Godly men can hardly step out of their homes and keep their minds pure. Whether they go to Wal-Mart, the gas station, or a restaurant, they face a potential spiritual battle in their minds. They should not have to fight that battle when they go to church–or wherever they happen to see you. One man, a believer, shared his battle with sensual thoughts with my husband. He said his battle was actually heightened when he went to church and saw Christian women dressed in a sensual manner–not with apparel appropriate for godly women.

We claim that the Bible is our only authority for faith and practice. However, so many times in our fashions we disregard that authority. We want to wear stylish clothing and be attractive; we want to wear clothes which the world deems fashionable. I believe that most women, including Christian women, have those feelings. To find the ultimate criterion for a Christian lady's dress, you must go to the Bible. You must be careful *whose* Designer Fashions you wear–God's or Satan's. Remember that clothing sends a message. As we study these Biblical principles, consider what message your clothing sends to others.

I. Your clothing must distinguish you as a woman.
II. Your clothing indicates your *perceived* character and relationships.
III. You must develop godly character.
IV. You must send the right message.

I. Your clothing must distinguish you as a woman.

    A. God created man and woman in distinct ways (Genesis 2).
        1. God created the man (*adam*) (v. 7).
            a. God formed (*yatsar*) "fashioned" the man.[89]
            b. God formed him "from the dust of the ground."
            c. God "breathed into his nostrils" the breath of life and he became a living soul.
        2. God created the woman (*ishshah*) (v. 23).[90]
            a. God made (*banah*) "built" the woman.[91]
            b. God made her from a rib of Adam's body.
            c. God brought Eve to Adam.
        3. God created man and woman different sexually.
        4. Principle: Since God created the woman to be different from the man, she must maintain that distinction. She must be feminine in her dress–not masculine!

    B. God gave man and woman distinct responsibilities.
        1. The man was to dress (*work*) the garden and keep (*keep, guard*) it (Gen. 2:15).[92]
        2. The woman was to fulfill her husband's needs (Gen. 2).
            a. She was to help him (vv. 18, 20).
            b. She was to complete him (vv. 20-24).
            c. She was to be his companion (v. 18).
        3. Both were to be fruitful, multiply, and replenish the earth (Gen. 1:28).
        4. Both were to have dominion over the earth–not worship it (Gen. 1:28).
        5. The man was to leave his father and mother and cleave to his wife (Gen. 2:25).
        6. Principle: Since God gave woman different responsibilities than man, she must maintain those distinctions in fulfilling her responsibilities.

    C. God made clothes for Adam and Eve–after they sinned (Gen. 3:21).
        1. After their creation they were naked–but they were *not* ashamed (Gen. 2:25).

  2. After their fall they were naked–and they *were* ashamed (Gen. 3:7).
   a. They realized they were naked, and they knew evil.
✦ You must choose "God's Designer Fashions"–not "Satan's Sensual Skimpy Creations."
   b. They tried to clothe themselves with aprons.
   c. Their nakedness separated them from God (Gen. 3:10).
    (1) They feared God.
    (2) They hid from God.
✦ They both felt the need to hide from God, though they had made themselves aprons.
✦ Scripture does not talk about being "half-naked." It just talks about nakedness. After Adam and Eve sinned, they made themselves aprons. The word *apron* has the idea of a girdle, loin cloth, etc. Even though they wore aprons (evidently covering the private reproductive parts of their bodies), *they* still considered themselves naked and hid from God. After God dealt with their sin, He clothed them with coats.
    (3) They realized their nakedness; God did not tell them they were naked.
   d. Their shame resulted from their disobedience to God's Word (Gen. 3:11).
  3. Principle: Nakedness results in shame.
  4. Principle: Disobedience results in shame and separation from God.

 D. God made them coats–not aprons (Gen. 3:21).
  1. God clothed them, even though they were husband and wife, alone in the world.
  2. God clothed them, lest they wander through the world naked and continue to feel the shame of nakedness.
   a. The word *coat* means:
    (1) "tunic, undergarment,
    (2) a long shirt-like garment, usually of linen."[93]
   b. The tunic would have had a high neckline.
   c. The tunic would have been long, most likely to the ankles.
   d. The tunic would have been loose-fitting.
✦ These garments were loose enough that they had to be *girded* in times of battle, running, working, etc.
   e. God's covering (coats) indicated that they were no longer naked.
   f. Adam and Eve made themselves aprons, but they were not sufficiently clothed until God made them coats.
  3. Principle: God's first criterion for clothing was distinctly different from man's criterion. It was "high, long and loose"–not "low, short, skimpy and clingy."
✦ It was high enough, long enough, and loose enough to prevent the exposure or emphasis of the private parts of the body.

 E. God gave examples of distinction in His Word.
  1. Joseph's *coat distinguished* him as Jacob's favorite son (Gen. 37:3).

- The coat, which Jacob's other sons did not have, was an identifying characteristic of Joseph's *relationship with his father*.

    2. Aaron's *coat distinguished* him as Israel's priest (Lev. 8:13).
- His coat was an identifying characteristic of his *position in Israel*. His sons also wore coats (Lev. 8:13), but other men in Israel did not wear those same coats.

    3. Tamar's *garment* (coat) *distinguished* her as a virgin daughter of King David (II Sam. 13:18).
- Tamar's coat was an identifying characteristic of her *character and relationships*.

    4. King Jehoshaphat's robe *distinguished* him as a king (II Ch. 18:28-31).
- King Ahab's clothing said, "I'm just a *soldier*." King Jehoshaphat's clothing said, "I'm the *king*." His clothing was an identifying characteristic *that he was a king*, the *only* king on the battle field. Therefore, he was the one to kill.

    5. Principle: Godly women's clothes *must distinguish them as pure, an identifying characteristic of their relationship with God.*

F. Application: _____

Not only does clothing distinguish you as a woman,

II. Your clothing indicates your *perceived* character and relationships.

    A. Tamar, Judah's daughter-in-law, understood this principle (Gen. 38:11-16).
- When Judah approached Tamar, she *spoke not a word* to him. However, Judah *saw her clothing and received the message she sent–he thought she was a harlot* (v. 15)! "And when Judah saw her, he thought her to be an harlot . . . because she had covered her face."
- What was Judah's reaction to Tamar's message sent by her clothing? He *assumed* she was inviting him to have sex with her. "And he turned unto her by the way, and said, 'Go to, I pray thee, let me come in unto thee (v. 16). . . .'" *Without speaking a word, Tamar invited Judah to have sex with her.*
- Tamar chose to *distinguish* herself, by her dress, as a harlot–though she was not a harlot. This was intentional. Her true identity was disguised. *Her clothing alone defined her perceived character. Judah was totally convinced she was a harlot!*
- Tamar's true identity and character were totally disguised by her dress.

    B. Tamar, King David's daughter, understood and fought for this principle (II Samuel 13:1-19).
- Amnon was King David's eldest son (I Ch. 3:1). Tamar, a virgin (v. 2), was King David's daughter and Amnon's half-sister. Absalom was Tamar's brother (I Ch. 3:4). Her virginity was evidenced by a garment (coat) that she wore, ". . . for with such robes were the king's daughters that were virgins appareled (v. 18)."
- Amnon forcibly raped his half-sister Tamar. Tamar took off her special coat which distinguished her as a virgin and tore it. She put ashes on her head and wept. Absalom took her to his house, where she remained desolate.
- Tamar did nothing to cause her devastating and shameful treatment.

    1. She dressed modestly; her clothing sent the right message.

    2. She obeyed her father, King David.

3. She tried to help her half-brother, who deceived her and stole her virginity.
4. She rejected all of her degraded half-brother's advances.

C. Principle: Godly women's clothing must distinguish them as pure, an identifying characteristic of their relationship with God. They must not wear anything that distinguishes them as sensual or enticing.

D. Application: _____

III. You must develop godly character.

A. Determine to remain pure (I Cor. 6:18-7:1; II Tim. 2:22).

✦ Dr. Charles Surrett, "When you give your purity to your husband, you never really give it away."[94]
   1. Establish and maintain your testimony of purity.
   2. Be sure your words (your verbal communication) and your dress (your nonverbal communication) send a godly message.

B. Develop prudence.
   1. Prudence is the ability to reason wisely, speak correctly, and live godly.
   2. Accept godly correction and instruction (Prov. 15:5).
   3. Ask the Lord to give you wisdom (James 1:5).
   4. Learn to analyze and evaluate a situation before making a decision (Prov. 22:3).
   5. Ask yourself the following questions in regard to your dress.
      a. "Does this clothing honor God or glorify Satan?"
      b. "Will this clothing cause a man to think sensual thoughts?"
      c. "Would I want to stand before the Lord in this clothing?"
   6. Do not be alone in isolated areas at night.

✦ If you are driving, be aware of where you are: the name of the highway, perhaps the town or city which is closest to your location. If a car pulls up behind you and the driver puts on his lights, acknowledge the driver by putting on your hazard lights and slowing down a little. If you are on an interstate highway you may call *47 (Highway Patrol). Almost all states recognize the *47 number as a direct link to state troopers.

✦ If you are not on the interstate, call 911. The dispatcher should then connect you to the nearest local police department. Tell the dispatcher where you are and ask the police dispatcher if there are any policemen in your area. The dispatcher can check to see if there are legitimate police cars in that area–even any unmarked police cars. If there is a legitimate policeman following you, tell the dispatcher that you are slowing down, you are not pulling away, and you will stop when you arrive at a well-lit gas station or safe place to stop. If it appears that the first area is almost deserted, it would be a good idea not to stop but to continue to look for another place. Policemen have to respect your right to keep driving to a safe and quiet place. However, you may still have to appear in court. Some of this information was provided by Captain Jerry Tessneer of the Kings Mountain Police Department, King Mountain, North Carolina on April 4, 2014.

   7. Do not be alone with a male who is not your father, brother, a trusted relative, or husband in private situations. Example: Dinah (Gen. 34:1)

C. Run from fornication (I Cor. 6:18; II Tim. 2:22).
   1. *Fornication* means ". . . illicit sexual intercourse."[95]
- Fornication is any sexual relationship outside of marriage. It includes pre-marital sex, incest, adultery, homosexuality, child molestation, etc.
   2. Fornication is a sin against one's own body.
   3. Do not make provision (forethought) for the flesh (Rom. 13:14).[96]
      a. Determine to have a no touch relationship with the opposite sex (I Cor. 7:1).
      b. Determine not to flirt (Prov. 6:25).
   4. Refrain from being "available" (Gen. 2:18-22; 3:16).
- Women who are easily available are less desirable!
      a. God knew Adam was alone, which was not good (Gen. 2:18).
      b. God knew Adam needed a helper (Gen. 2:20).
      c. God made Eve and brought her to Adam (Gen. 2:20-22).

D. Principle: Godly character and prudence help retain purity and are sources of protection.

E. Application: _____
_____

IV. You must send the right message.

A. Believe that all observed behavior sends a message (Lk. 6:46; I John 1:6).
- "Personal apparel represents deliberate choices and is a guide to personality. How we dress . . . shows sexual attraction and sexual interest, group identification, status, identification of role, and expression of self-concept."[97]
- You must understand the three laws of involuntary nonverbal communication: (1) You cannot not communicate; (2) Involuntary nonverbal messages most readily communicate your emotions, attitudes, relationships; (3) Your involuntary nonverbal messages are often of high validity.[98]
- Even "The heavens declare the glory of God; and the firmament showeth his handiwork (Ps. 19:1)." You are a part of God's handiwork, a woman uniquely created by God. Your clothing should be an evidence of your Divine design as a woman. God, the All-wise, Almighty Creator, has given you His criteria for His Designer clothes.

B. Do not arouse men's passions with immodest dress, because men are aroused by sight (I Tim. 2:9-10).
- To arouse a man's passions and then say, "No, I don't want to have sex" is like a man telling a woman he loves her in order to have sex, though he has no intentions of marrying her.

C. Obey and glorify God, not yourself; follow His guidelines for your clothing (I Cor. 10:31; I Tim. 2:9-10).
- God set the guidelines for clothing restraints far enough away from the private bodily areas in order to protect a person's privacy and purity.
   1. High enough so your breasts are not exposed at any time (Gen. 3:21)

- The space between the top of your top, blouse, dress, etc., and your collarbone should not be more than two to three fingers width. Wearing tops lower than that draws attention away from your face to your bosom, even if your cleavage is not displayed.

2. Loose enough so that your breasts are not emphasized (Gen. 3:21)

- Clothing should not accentuate the private areas of your body. God's first criterion for clothing was different from man's criterion. It was "high enough, loose enough, and long enough," not "low-cut, clingy, and short." The virtuous woman "girded" her clothing in preparation for work (Prov. 31:17). This indicates that her garment was flowing, loose. It had to be tied with a belt of some kind in order for her to be able to work efficiently. The standard set by God was to refrain from accentuating the private areas of the body.
- Personal hint: Take hold of your outer clothing (dress, blouse, top, skirt, etc), and lift it up slightly. Does it fall into place with ease? That seems to be the idea conveyed by a tunic.

3. Long enough so your thighs are covered at all times (Gen. 3:21; Ex. 28:42)

- In order to insure that your thighs are covered at all times, it would be best to make sure your knees are covered at all times.

4. Modest (I Tim. 2:9)

- *Modest* apparel is "orderly, well-arranged, decent, modest . . . in its primary sense as 'harmonious arrangement, adornment. . . .'"[99]
- *Modest apparel* does not pertain merely to non-sensual clothing. Your appearance should be orderly, not having the appearance of disorder. Disorder draws more attention than does order and it causes confusion. It does not send a clear message.

5. Respectful (I Tim. 2:9)

    a. *Shamefacedness* is ". . . a sense of shame, honor, modesty, bashfulness, reverence, regard for others, respect. . . . having regard to others, respectfulness,
 . . . is that modesty which is rooted in character,
 . . . would always restrain a good man from an unworthy act."[100]

    b. There are two Greek words for *shame*.

Aidos = idos - "shamefacedness"	*Aischune* = eiskuna - "shame"
Feeling of innate moral repugnance to doing a dishonorable act	Moral repugnance not found, but rather a feeling of disgrace from doing an unworthy thing–or fear of disgrace which serves to prevent its being done.
Nobler word	Having regard chiefly to the opinions of others
Fear of doing a shameful thing	Chiefly a fear of being caught
Would always restrain a good man from an unworthy act	Might restrain a bad one from an unworthy act[101]

    c. *Shamefacedness* is not just a fear of being caught dressing dishonorably ("breaking the rule"), but it is the inward character which restrains you from dressing in a way that dishonors God, yourself, and others.

- As a godly woman, you must show respect through your dress to God and your male head, who is either your father if you are unmarried, or your husband if you are married. When selecting clothing to purchase to wear publicly, ask yourself, "Does this clothing show respect to God, and to my father or my husband? Will it bring them shame? Will it cause *any* man to have sensual thoughts?" Determine to *honor God* with your dress–not *arouse the passions* of a man. If you can dress fashionably, and not violate Biblical principles, that is certainly acceptable. You must not let your thoughtless, selfish desire to be fashionable, regardless of Biblical principles, shame you, others, or those who love you.

Let your clothes enhance–not detract from–your profession of godliness.

    d. *Shamefacedness* is a source of protection.
- Dressing with respect for yourself and others not only honors the LORD, keeps your male head from shame, helps godly men in their struggle to keep their minds pure, but it is also a source of protection for you. A policeman in Gastonia, North Carolina ". . . recommended women out jogging try to avoid wearing revealing clothing."[102] If you choose to dress immodestly or seductively, you are opening yourself up to danger.

  6. Sound judgment (I Tim. 2:9)
    a. *Sobriety* is ". . . soundness of mind . . . 'sound judgment' practically expresses the meaning. . . ."[103]
    b. "'. . . It is that habitual inner self-judgment, with its constant rein on all the passions and desires, which would hinder the temptation to these from arising. . . .'"[104]

  7. Not unnecessarily expensive (I Tim. 2:9)
    a. Not with gold or pearls
    b. Not with costly array means "primarily, 'the very end or limit' . . . with reference to price, of highest 'cost,' very expensive . . . raiment. . . . (I Tim. 2:9)"[105]

- ". . . There is one general rule . . . that the true line is passed when more is thought of this external adorning, than of the ornament of the heart."[106]
- The inner meek and quiet spirit is, in God's sight, of great price (I Pet. 3:4). The same word is used for *costly array* (I Tim. 2:9), in regard to *outward apparel*, and for *great price* (I Pet. 3:4), in regard to the *inner meek and quiet spirit*. It has the idea of "excellent, of surpassing value." In both I Timothy and I Peter God discourages the wearing of very expensive outward apparel. In I Timothy, women are exhorted to let their outward adornment be modest–not costly–accompanied by good works. In I Peter, God encourages the development of an inner meek and quiet spirit, which is extremely valuable in God's sight.

We must regard very highly what God declares to be "of the highest cost"
–not what man regards as most fashionable.

  8. Feminine (I Timothy 2:10; Deut. 22:5)
- "The woman shall not wear that which pertaineth unto a man, neither shall a man put on a woman's garment: for all that do so are abomination unto the LORD thy God (Deut. 22:5)."
- The word for *woman* is *naw-sheem* which means "woman, wife, female."[107]
- The phrase *"shall not wear that which pertaineth"* is the word *kel ee* which means "article, vessel, implement, utensil."[108]
- The word for *man* is not *adam,* but *gheh-ber* which means "man, strong man, warrior, emphasizing strength or ability to fight."[109]

      a. A woman's clothing should be a tool to demonstrate the softness and femininity of her gender.[110]
      b. A man's clothing should be a tool to demonstrate the strength of his gender.[111]
      c. It is an abomination to diminish the distinctions between sexes.

- 'The woman shall not wear that which pertaineth unto a man, neither shall a man put on a woman's garment' . . . for the adoption of the habiliments of the one sex by the other is an outrage on decency, obliterates the distinctions of nature by fostering softness and effeminacy in the man, impudence and boldness in the woman as well as levity and hypocrisy in both; and, in short, it opens the door to an influx of so many evils that all who wear the dress of another sex are pronounced 'an abomination unto the Lord.'[112] (Sic)

  9. Appropriate (I Tim. 2:10)
      a. It is appropriate for a woman who professes godliness and does good works.

- Works which support godliness should be part of a Christian woman's adornment.

      b. It should be appropriate for the occasion.

- If you are not sure whether the clothing, shoes, etc. are appropriate, ask yourself, *"For what occasion or purpose was this article of clothing made?"*

It is inappropriate for the virtuous woman to dress like the strange woman.

      c. It is distinguished by good works, not external decorations, which support your profession of godliness (I Tim. 2:10).

- The works of Rebekah, Ruth, Hannah, Priscilla, and Lydia were becoming to their professed faith in God.
- A woman cannot accomplish good when she disregards the harmful effect her clothing may have on others, especially men. Causing a man, whether saved or unsaved, to think sensual thoughts is the work of Satan–not of Christ. A woman must not strive to have the most expensive clothes, nor spend excessive time on her appearance. These draw attention to *herself*, not to *Christ*. Everything about her appearance sends a message, which must *agree* with her profession of godliness in order to display good works. Trying to do good works while dressing for Satan is counterproductive. It does not accomplish good, but in reality it supports the cause of Satan.

  10. Indicates honor, the clothing of the virtuous woman (Prov. 31:22)

- "She maketh herself coverings of tapestry; her clothing *is* silk and purple."
  –*Silk* is something "bleached white, byssus, fine linen, linen."[113]
  –*Purple* is the color "purple, red purple."[114]

      a. The first mention of *silk* ("linen") was when Joseph was honored and dressed in a garment of linen (Gen. 41:42).

- Principle of first mention: The first time a word is mentioned in Scripture gives a clue to how the term is to be interpreted in the rest of the Bible.

      b. Linen was Pharaoh's choice of fabric to clothe Joseph when he elevated him (Gen. 41:42).
      c. Linen was God's choice of fabric to make many items for the tabernacle and the priests' clothing (Exodus).

- The word is mentioned thirty times in Exodus concerning the Tabernacle, its furnishings, and the priestly garments. It would have been a sin for the priests to refuse to wear the clothing God designed for them.
    - (1) The tabernacle was the place where Israel was commanded to sacrifice and worship God.
    - (2) Many times both the words *linen* and *purple* are mentioned.
      - d. Linen was Ahasuerus' choice of fabric to make the cords for the hangings in his palace at Shushan (Es. 1:6).
      - e. Linen was Ahasuerus' choice of fabric for the royal apparel for Mordecai, after he promoted him (Es. 8:15).
      - f. Linen and silk were God's choice of fabrics to clothe Israel to elevate her and make her beautiful (Ezek. 16:10, 13).
      - g. David, the Levites, and singers wore linen when returning the Ark to its rightful place (I Ch. 15:27).
      - h. Linen was the virtuous woman's choice of fabric for clothing, the woman whose value is "far above rubies" (Prov. 31:10, 22).

It is sinful, and possibly dangerous, for the virtuous woman to dress as strange woman.

11. Attractive, God's clothing for Israel (Ezek. 16:1-18)
    a. God raised Israel to honor.
        (1) Figuratively, He found Israel as a naked baby.
        (2) He cleansed her and made a covenant with her.
        (3) He clothed her with expensive, beautiful clothing and jewelry.
        (4) He prospered her with a kingdom.
        (5) The beauty God gave her was perfect.
- True beauty comes from God.
    b. **But** Israel decided to trust in her own beauty (v. 15).
        (1) Israel played the harlot.
        (2) Israel made idols of the jewels and clothing God gave her.

D. Principle: One's clothing indicates one's perceived character and group identification.
- Examples of clothing and group identification: Military, Policemen, Firemen, Sports teams, etc.

E. Application: _____
_____

Remember that God uniquely designed you as a woman. Your clothing must distinguish you as a woman. Even the world recognizes this principle in some ways. God wants you to dress in His Designer Clothes every day! The Bible teaches that *all* women should be distinct from *men* in their dress, and *godly* women should also be distinct from *sensual* fashion in their dress.

Your clothing indicates your perceived character and relationships. Tamar, Judah's daughter-in-law, and Tamar, David's daughter, both understood this. Without speaking a word, Judah's daughter-in-law Tamar enticed him with her clothing. Despite her pure dress and desperate determination to retain her purity, King David's daughter Tamar was stripped of her virginity by her degraded half-brother Amnon.

You must develop godly character. Determine to remain pure; maintain a no touch policy with the opposite sex. Develop prudence, which is the ability to reason wisely, speak correctly, and live godly. In order to be prudent, you must heed the warnings of the wise. Then you will learn to foresee dangerous and evil situations, and avoid them at all cost. Run from situations which could lead to sexual impurity.

Remember that all observed behavior sends a message. You must send the right message. What do your clothes say about you?

"Look at me! I want to be noticed!"

"Look at me! I have an attractive body!"

"Look at me, world. I look just like you! But I do want you to listen to me, because I want to tell you how you can go to heaven. Yes, I'm going to heaven, but right now I want to look just like you."

"Look at me! I'm in style!"

"Look at me! I'm available!"

God commands you to dress in His Designer Clothes every day!

1. High enough so your breasts are not exposed at any time (Gen. 3:21)
2. Loose enough so that your breasts are not emphasized (Gen. 3:21)
3. Long enough to cover your thighs at all times (Gen. 3:21; Ex. 28:42)
4. Modest (having the idea of orderliness) (I Tim. 2:9)
5. Respectful, the character quality which restrains you from dressing sensually (I Tim. 2:9)
6. Sound judgement (I Tim. 2:9)
7. Not unnecessarily expensive (I Tim. 2:9)
8. Feminine (I Tim. 2:10; Deut. 22:5)
9. Appropriate, which supports your professed relationship with the Lord and is appropriate for the occasion (I Tim. 2:10)
10. Displays honor (Prov. 31:22)
11. Attractive (Ezek. 16:1-18)

We have learned that linen was God's choice of fabric to clothe Israel. In Ezekiel He recounted her history. Figuratively, God found Israel as a naked baby, cleansed her, made a covenant with her, clothed her with expensive, beautiful clothing and jewelry, and prospered her with a kingdom. God raised Israel to honor. The beauty God gave to Israel was perfect. They were God's chosen people.

But, Israel decided to trust in her own beauty. She played the harlot and shamefully made idols of the jewels and clothing God had graciously given her. Have you ever said to the LORD, "Thank you for all you have done for me. I'll go where you want me to go, I'll say what you want me to say–but please, don't ask me to wear what you want me to wear?" To refuse God's guidelines for your clothing is rebellion against the Lord. Rebellion led Israel into spiritual fornication and idolatry.

Remember Tamar, Judah's daughter-in-law. She spoke not a word, but Judah assumed by her dress she was a harlot, desirous of sex! He then acted upon the information he received.

Do not dress like Tamar! Christian women must choose to obey, honor, and glorify God by following His criteria for their clothing. Your clothing must distinguish you ("make you worthy of respect") as a godly woman because of your relationship with the LORD. In order to have an effective Christian testimony, your clothing must say, "I don't belong to the world. I am a Christian–I belong to Christ." You are one of God's chosen people (I Pet. 2:9).

How do you want God to *see* you? What do you want others to *think* of you?

Determine to remain pure. Defilement will likely occur without a prior commitment to purity. (Daniel 1:8) The higher degree of purity you desire, the greater abhorrence of defilement you will have.

Chapter Ten

The Help Meet's Ten Commandments - "Right Choices - Real Happiness"

- ✦ Scripture: John 13:17
- ✦ Principle: You must know and obey God's commandments in order to do good for your husband.
- ✦ John 13:17: "If ye know these things, happy are ye if ye do them."

According to Tammy Fay Bakker, "The way to keep a husband happy is to flirt with him, wear plenty of makeup and be unpredictable."[115] What foolish and empty advice! Her advice appeared in a book called *Christian Wives–Women Behind the Evangelists Reveal Their Faith in Modern Marriage*.

Mrs. Bakker made some very wrong assumptions. Wrong assumptions, whether made out of ignorance or disobedience, bring disastrous results. Let's see what Tammy's advice means. *Flirt* means to "behave amorously without serious intent."[116] A wife would be a temptress, not a completer. *Unpredictable* means "unable to declare something in advance."[117] An unpredictable wife would be untrustworthy, unreliable, have little worth, and do evil to her husband. Make-up is a *cosmetic,* an "external application intended to beautify the complexion."[118] A wife who depends upon her temporary *external* beauty will not determine to develop the *internal* meek and quiet spirit. Strong, stable marriages have never been built on worldly philosophies or techniques; they must be established on the Word of God (Proverbs 24:3-4).

The "Cinderella and Prince Charming happily ever after marriage" does not exist!

How can a wife build a good relationship with her husband and a strong marriage? She must understand God's principles regarding marriage in order to be the helper, completer, and companion that God uniquely created her to be. Not only must she *know* what the Bible says–she must choose to *obey* It. "If ye know these things, happy are ye if ye do them (John 13:17)." This will not guarantee her husband's happiness–or contentment. Each person must make his or her own choices. *However, she will do good for her husband and be blessed by the Lord.*

I. A help meet must do good for her husband by being a virtuous woman.
II. A help meet must accept God's role for her–a helper to her husband.
III. A help meet must captivate her husband and become his completer.
IV. A help meet must be her husband's companion, walking in agreement with him.
V. A help meet must love her husband, desiring him alone.

VI. A help meet must submit to her husband, accepting God's design for order in marriage.
VII. A help meet must be a diligent, wise home builder.
VIII. A help meet must honor her husband with prudence.
IX. A help meet must choose to reverence her husband, in order to be a good example to their children.
X. A help meet must fulfill her husband's needs, which gives him security.

I. A help meet must do good for her husband by being a virtuous woman (Proverbs 31:10-12).

    A. A wife must have the character of a virtuous woman (Prov. 31:10-31; 12:4; Ruth 3:11).
        1. She is a woman of strength (vv. 13-17).
        2. She has the ability to serve, which is character, not talent (vv. 13-27).
        3. She is a woman of moral worth (v. 30), in contrast to the strange woman (Prov. 2:16-17; 5:7; 7:10-21).
            a. The virtuous woman fears the Lord, which establishes her moral worth (v. 30).
            b. The strange woman is rebellious toward God, destitute of moral worth (2:16-17).
            c. The virtuous woman's moral worth is evidenced by her unselfish concern for others (31:13-27).
            d. The strange woman's lack of moral worth is evidenced by her self-centered focus (Prov. 7:10-21).
        4. She is different from the world–she is rare (v. 10).
- Different in character: virtuous; different in service: unselfish; different in clothing: honorable; different in focus: family and others; different in motivation: diligent, not lazy; different in values: giving, not taking; different in speech: speaks with wisdom and kindness, not gossip, slander, or harshness.
- She has made different choices, because she is godly in character, unselfish in her focus.
        5. She is highly-treasured (v. 10).

    B. A wife must follow the example of Ruth (Ruth 1-4).
        1. Ruth was from an ungodly nation called the Moabites (1:4).
        2. Ruth became virtuous in God's sight through salvation, choosing to trust in God (1:16; 2:12).
        3. Ruth became virtuous in man's sight.
            a. She established a testimony of godly character (3:11).
            b. She established a testimony of unselfish service, choosing to serve Naomi (1:16-17; 2:2).
                (1) The servant recognized her strength and diligence (2:7).
                (2) Boaz recognized her ability to serve (2:11).
                (3) Boaz and the people of Bethlehem recognized her moral worth (3:11).
                She was self-motivated (2:2).

> She was humble, willing to glean, which was reserved for the poor (2:2).
> She was diligent (2:7).

C. A wife must accept Christ as her Savior, thereby establishing her virtuous character in God's sight; she must then establish a testimony of godly character in man's sight.

D. A wife must do good for her husband, regardless of his character.

E. Application: _____

II. A help meet must accept God's role for her–a helper to her husband (Genesis 2:18-24).

A. God created Eve for Adam, not Adam for Eve (Gen. 2:22-24; I Cor. 11:8-9).

B. God established her responsibilities to her husband.
1. Help her husband (Prov. 31:10-31)
    a. Valuable helper, v. 10
    b. Trustworthy helper, v. 11
    c. Beneficial helper, v. 12
    d. Self-motivated helper, vv. 13, 27
    e. Industrious helper, vv. 14-24
    f. Sacrificial helper, v. 15
    g. Purposeful helper, v. 16
    h. Prepared helper, vv. 17, 21
    i. Successful helper, v. 18
    j. Example to others to others, v. 19
    k. Generous helper, v. 20
    l. Attractive helper, v. 22
    m. Honorable helper, vv. 23-25
    n. Wise and kind helper, v. 26
    o. Prudent helper, v. 27
    p. Praise-worthy helper, vv. 28–31
    q. God-fearing helper, v. 30
    r. Rewarded helper, vv. 25, 31
2. Complete her husband (Gen. 2:20-24)
3. Be a companion to her husband (Gen. 2:18)

C. God demands a response to his plan.
1. Eve responded with refusal, evidence of a proud spirit (Gen. 3:5-6).

Discontentment–if not dealt with–leads to more sin!
Eve "walked in the counsel of the ungodly" and paid a great price (Gen. 3:7-24).

2. Mary responded with acceptance, evidence of a humble spirit (Luke 1:38).

Mary accepted God's Word and was highly praised (Lk. 1:42, 48).

D. A wife must choose to become her husband's helper.

E. Application: _____

III. A help meet must captivate her husband and become his completer (Genesis 1:27-28; Proverbs 5:18-19; I Cor. 7:1-5).

    A. God's three purposes for the sexual relationship are:
        1. Procreation (Gen. 1:27-28)
        2. Pleasure (Prov. 5:15-19)
        3. Prevention of illicit sex (I Cor. 7:5)

✦ This is God's ordained physical oneness between the husband and his wife.

    B. The marriage relationship legitimately fulfills all three purposes.

    C. Physical oneness is to be fulfilled only within the boundary of marriage between a man and a woman (Gen. 2:24; Prov. 5:17; Heb. 13:4).

    D. Physical oneness within marriage is not shameful, but it is private (Gen. 2:25).

    E. Physical oneness fulfilled legitimately helps prevent fornication (I Cor. 7:2).

    F. Physical oneness may be abstained from temporarily by mutual agreement (I Cor. 7:5).

    G. Physical oneness must be re-established to avoid fornication (I Cor. 7:5).

    H. All other sexual relationships are unholy and will be judged by God (Heb. 13:4).

    I. A wife must choose to captivate her husband (Prov. 5:19; I Cor. 7:3).

    J. Application: _____

IV. A help meet must be her husband's companion, walking in agreement with him (Malachi 2:14).

    A. The word *companion* refers ". . . to the very close bond that can exist between two people."[119]

B. Adam was alone, which God said was not good (Gen. 2:18).

C. God made Eve to be Adam's companion.
   1. Adam and Eve were to become one–have union.
   2. Adam and Eve were to enjoy fellowship–have a close bond.
      a. A wife must make her husband her best friend!
      b. A wife must learn to enjoy what he enjoys.
      c. A wife must set aside time to spend with just him.
   3. Adam and Eve had to agree to have true unity (Amos 3:3).

D. A wife must choose to have unity and fellowship with her husband.
   1. She must choose to submit to his authority.
   2. She must choose to follow his leadership.
   3. She may humbly appeal to him about a decision he is considering.

✦ Follow the example of Queen Esther. She appealed to her husband, King Ahasuerus, without dishonoring him, though he had unknowingly signed a decree that allowed for the extinction of her people (Es. 3:5-15). Even he could not change his decree (Es. 4:1-8:6). If a wife chooses to appeal, she must do it with a humble spirit. If she appeals and her husband does not change his mind, she must honor his leadership, while ultimately trusting in the Lord. If she believes it is the wrong decision–she can pray! God can change her husband's mind, the situation, or allow them to learn a valuable lesson.

✦ Most of the times when I did not agree, but left the decision with my husband, he was almost always right. He had the character to proceed, in spite of my appeal to change his decision.

E. The atmosphere in the home should be sweet and refreshing for those who dwell there, helping to produce unity (Ps. 133:1).
   1. Unity begins with God and descends to man.
   2. Unity is not natural for man, but it is for God.
   3. Disunity is undesirable and unpleasant for the family (Eccl. 4:6).
   4. Disunity will lead to division (Matt. 12:25).
   5. A wife must be a companion–not a combatant.

*Does your spirit refresh and unite people,
or does it irritate and divide those who live in your home?*

F. Application: _____
_____

V. A help meet must love her husband, desiring him alone (Genesis 3:16).

A. Adam had been alone with no one to desire him or love him.

B. The criteria for godly love is selflessness (I Cor. 13).

1. Words without action are not valid (v. 1).
2. Service without love is vanity (v. 2).
3. Sacrifice without love is unprofitable (v. 3).
4. Love is kind (v. 4).
5. Love is not easily provoked (v. 5).
6. Love rejoices in the truth (v. 6).
7. Love bears all things (v. 7).
8. Love is unending (v. 8).
9. Love is unequaled in value (v. 13).
10. Love is not based on a feeling–it is a choice .
    (a) A wife must learn what pleases her husband; if it is godly, then she must determine to please him.
    (b) A wife must remain attractive to him and for him.
    (c) A wife must express her thanks for his help in projects.
    (d) A wife must not greet him with complaints when he arrives home!
    (e) A wife must be faithful to him.
    (f) A wife must thank him for working to provide for their family.
    (g) A wife must express her love in words and actions (I John 4:18).

"Love can be known only from the actions it prompts."[120]

C. A wife must choose to love her husband and fulfill her marriage vows to him.

D. Application: _____

VI. A help meet must submit to her husband, thereby accepting God's design for order in marriage (Ephesians 5:22).

A. God commanded the husband to rule his wife (Gen. 3:16; Eph. 5:23-24).

B. God commanded the wife to submit to her husband (Gen. 3:16; Eph. 5:22).
   1. In Creation, Adam was formed first (I Tim. 2:13).
   2. In the Fall, Eve was deceived (I Tim. 2:14).

C. Submission is a commandment for all wives (I Pet. 3:1).

D. *Submission* means to "arrange yourself in rank under."[121]

E. Submission is an attitude manifested by a meek and quiet spirit (I Pet. 3:3-4).

F. Submission is based on a trust in God (I Pet. 3:5).

G. Submission is so important that God said it is better for a man to remain single than to

have a contentious wife (Prov. 21:9, 19; 25:24).
- ✦ Contentious means "desiring to rule in every aspect of the government–make, interpret, and enforce the laws."[122]
- ✦ It is sad that God said it is better for a contentious woman's husband to be alone. He had said in the beginning that it was *not good* for the man to be alone (Gen. 2:18).

H. Submission is so effective that God said an unsaved husband can be won to the Lord by it (I Pet. 3:1-2).

I. Refusal to submit to her husband's Scriptural authority is rebellion against the Lord.
   1. A wife is not obligated to disobey Scripture, if commanded to do so.
   2. Most likely, a wife's refusal to submit rarely involves a command to disobey Scripture.

J. Contention and submission were both illustrated by Sarah (Gen. 16:1-6; I Pet. 3:6).

K. A wife must choose to submit to her husband by an act of her will–not her emotions (I Pet. 3:5).

L. Application: _____
_____

VII. A help meet must be a diligent, wise home builder (Proverbs 14:1).

A. A help meet must be willing to build her home by bearing children, if God wills (Prov. 14:1; Gen. 16:2).
- ✦ Much of our society is willing to enjoy the pleasure of the sexual relationship, but they do not want the responsibility of bearing and caring for the children conceived as a result of their relationships. God said that every wise woman builds her house. This can be accomplished through childbearing and wisely managing her home.

B. A help meet must build her home by working diligently (Prov. 31:12-27)!
   1. She does good for her husband (v. 12).
   2. She works willingly (vv. 13, 18-19).
   3. She prepares food (vv. 14-15).
   4. She purchases wisely (vv. 16, 24).
   5. She cares for the poor and needy (v. 20).
- ✦ The godly wife recognizes their needs and reaches out to them. She helps those who cannot reciprocate. She is the initiator, reaching out to them; they are not reaching out to her.
   6. She provides clothing for her household (vv. 21-22).
   7. She guides and guards the ways of her household (v. 27).
   8. She is industrious–not lazy (v. 27).

C. A help meet must build her family by speaking wisely and kindly (v. 26; Prov. 16:24).

D. A help meet must choose to serve, not to be served.

E. A help meet must plan purposeful activity and inactivity.

F. A help meet's focus must be people–not possessions.

G. Application: _____
   _____

VIII. A help meet must honor her husband with prudence (Proverbs 31:26; 19:14).

A. Prudence is the ability to reason wisely, speak correctly, and live godly.

B. Prudence is obtained by:
   1. knowing the Lord (Prov. 19:14),
   2. accepting reproof (Prov. 15:5),
   3. studying the Word (Prov. 4:1-7; Ps. 19:7),
   4. applying the Word (James 1:25).

C. Esther honored her husband, King Ahasuerus (Esther 4-7).
   1. Esther did not usurp his authority (5:4-8).

✦ In spite of impending, extreme danger for her herself and her nation, Esther did not usurp her husband's authority. She did not connive or deceive to get her way, as wicked Haman had done.

      a. She fasted (4:16).
      b. She presented herself correctly (5:1-2).
      c. She presented her request humbly (5:4).
      d. She surrendered the results to God (4:16).
   2. The results were beneficial.
      a. Haman was exposed and punished (7:5-10).
      b. Israel was preserved (9:1-3).
      c. Mordecai was promoted (10:1-3).
      d. Ahasuerus was saved from a curse (Gen. 12:3).
   3. Esther's request was granted, but her husband was *not dishonored* in the process.

D. Sarai dishonored her husband, Abram (Gen. 16:1-6).
   1. Sarai was discontent with God's plan and timing in regard to her barrenness (vv. 1-2).
   2. Sarai usurped authority and commanded he commit adultery (vv. 1-2).
   3. Abram hearkened to Sarai (vv. 2-3).

God's perfect will does not begin in the mind of man–nor does it contradict God's Word.

   4. The results were destructive.

                a. The roles were reversed.
                    (1) Sarai: leader, not Abram's helper, completer, or companion
                    (2) Abram: follower, not Sarai's leader
                    (3) Hagar: Abram's helper/completer, not Sarai's handmaid.
                b. The handmaid conceived and despised ("rejected") Sarai.
                c. The relationships were changed.
                    (1) Hagar and Sarai's relationship changed.
                    (2) Hagar and Abram's relationship changed.

Sin changes relationships-sometimes in ways which may never be reversed- or are very difficult to fully restore.

                d. There has been unending conflict between Sarai and Hagar's sons and their descendants.
            5. **Sarai's command was carried out, but her husband was *dishonored* in the process.**

    E. A wife must choose to be prudent by reasoning wisely, speaking correctly, and living godly.

    F. Application: _____
    _____

IX. **A help meet must choose to reverence her husband, in order to be a good example to their children (Ephesians 5:33).**

    A. The word *reverence* means "to show reverential fear."[123]

    B. The word *reverence*, according to the dictionary, means "deep respect".

    C. The wife who fears the Lord will obey Him (Deut. 5:29).

    D. The wife, who rightly fears and submits to her husband, will be a good example for their children.

    E. The wife who reverences her husband will do good for her husband, her children, and herself!

    F. The wife who criticizes her husband dishonors him and weakens his leadership.
        1. Her criticism is harmful to their marriage and to their children.
        2. Disagreements between husband and wife must be settled privately.

    G. The wife must choose to reverence her husband's position, regardless of his character, and choose to serve him.

H. Application: _____

X. A help meet must fulfill her husband's needs, which gives him security (Proverbs 31:11).

A. The word *trust* expresses a "sense of well-being and security which results from having someone or something in whom to place confidence."[124]

B. The trust of a husband in his wife is the only human relationship in which trust is commended.[125]

C. The word *spoils* means "plunder"[126] (women, children, cattle, and valuable goods taken by the victors of war).

D. The husband's needs must be his wife's first earthly priority; she must be his helper, completer, and companion (Prov. 31:11).

E. The husband can be secure, if his wife chooses to fulfill his needs.
   1. She must choose to fulfill his physical needs as his homemaker.
   2. She must choose to fulfill his emotional needs as his best friend.
   3. She must choose to fulfill his sexual needs as his captivator.

F. Application: _____

Remember, the way to build a strong marriage is to follow God's instructions in His Word. "Through wisdom is an house builded; and by understanding it is established: And by knowledge shall the chambers be filled with all precious and pleasant riches (Proverbs 24:3-4)." *As a wife obeys God's commandments, she can help build a happy home, doing good for her husband, each day of her life.*

Becoming a virtuous woman will give her the *strength* to do good for her husband. She will be more valuable than any earthy riches he may ever obtain. Lack of godly character will bring him shame.

Accepting God's role will fulfill God's *purpose* for her, and provide a *helper* for her husband. If she refuses to fulfill her purpose, she becomes a hindrance, not a helper.

Captivating her husband can enable him to *complete* himself and *legitimately* fulfill and enjoy his God-given sexual desire. She can help him resist temptation by fulfilling his needs and praying for his resolve to remain morally pure. Refusal to captivate him will leave him vulnerable to unfaithfulness, pornography, etc.

Becoming her husband's companion, his best friend, walking in agreement with him, and **loving him** can *strengthen* their relationship and his leadership. If she fails to love him, become his best friend, and walk in agreement with him, she will probably become his critical combatant.

Submitting to her husband can also *strengthen* his leadership and *unite* their family. It may even bring an unsaved husband to Christ. Displaying a contentious spirit may drive him from her.

Building her home through child-bearing, if God permits, and diligently working in her home, can *satisfy* the needs of their family and many others. Slothfulness and/or a refusal to bear children will tear down, rather than build, her home and marriage.

Reasoning, speaking and living wisely will *honor* her husband and help *prevent* evil. Lack of prudence will leave her, and perhaps her husband, open to danger.

Reverencing her husband will also *honor* him and teach their children to do likewise. Her failure to hold her husband in high esteem may cause her husband to seek that esteem elsewhere. It may also influence their children to fail to regard their father or his authority with high esteem.

Fulfilling his needs can give her husband a *sense of security*. He will be able to *safely trust* in her–needing no one else! Failure to provide that sense of security may influence her husband to seek it elsewhere!

If she follows God's instructions, she will be rewarded. She will glorify God and may receive praise from her husband and their children. In fact, her works may praise her publicly. It is in serving that she will find satisfaction! "The special gift and ability of each creature defines its special limitation . . . the woman who accepts her limitations of womanhood finds in those very limitations her gift, her special calling . . . which bear her up into perfect freedom, into the will of God."[127]

A wife must obey God's Word in order to do good for her husband. These commands each necessitate a choice. A wife must make the right choices. Remember, sin changes relationships–sometimes in ways which may never be reversed or are very difficult to restore. The wrong choices made by Eve, Sarai, Lot's wife, Jezebel, Vashti, and Zeresh all affirm this principle.

A wife must determine to make sure that it would not be better for her husband to be alone–she must love and serve him with all her heart!

WORKS CITED

Adams, Jay E. *Christian Living in the Home.* Phillipsburg, NJ.: Presbyterian and Reformed Publishing Company, 1972.

Brooks, William D., Robert W. Heath. *Speech Communication.* Madison, WI.: WBC Brown and Benchmark Publishers, 1993.

Burkett, Larry. *"The World's Easiest Guide" to Finances.* Chicago: Northfield Publishing, 2000.

Elliot, Elisabeth. *Let Me Be A Woman.* Wheaton, IL.: Tyndale House Publishers, Inc., 1986.

Forward, Dr. Susan, Joan Torres. *Men Who Hate Women and the Women that Love Them.* Toronto: Bantam Books, 1986.

Gastonia Policeman. Gastonia, NC.: *Gaston Gazette*, 1 July 1993.

George, Elizabeth. *Beautiful in God's Eyes.* Eugene, OR.: Harvest House Publishers, 1998.

Harris, J. R. Ed., Gleason L. Archer, Jr., asst. ed., and Bruce K. Waltke, asst. ed. *Theological Wordbook of the Old Testament.* Vol. 1, 2. Chicago: Moody Press, 1980.

_____. "Headed for Divorce?" Gaston Gazette, 15 January 1993.

Jessup, Earl. Sermon preached at Ambassador Baptist College, January, 1995, Shelby, NC.

Langton, Sherry. "One Woman's Story," *Today's Christian Woman,* Jan/Feb, 1996.

_____. *Light For My Path.* Unionville, OH.: Barbour Publishing Co., 1999.

Mollenkamp, Becky. "Learning From Home School Families," *Better Homes and Gardens*, August 2002.

Online Bible Edition 2.10.09.

Schaffer, James and Colleen Todd. *Christian Wives–Women Behind the Evangelists Reveal Their Faith in Modern Marriage.* Garden City, NY: Doubleday, 1987.

Surrett, Dr. Charles L. Sermon preached at Emmanuel Baptist Church, Kings Mountain, NC., 10 August 2008.

Tonn, Maryjane Hooper, ed. *A Mother is Love.* Milwaukee: Ideals Publishing Corp., 1976.

Vine, W. E., Merrill F. Unger, and William White, EDS. *An Expository Dictionary of Biblical Words.* Nashville, TN.: Thomas Nelson Publishers, 1985.

_____. *Webster's Clear Type Dictionary.* Nashville, TN.: Thomas Nelson, Inc., 1976.

NOTES

1. W. E. Vine, Merrill F. Unger, and William White, EDS, *An Expository Dictionary of Biblical Words,* 2 vol. in one (Nashville, TN: Thomas Nelson Publishers, 1985), vol. 2, 62.

2. Ibid., 484.

3. Ibid., vol. 2, 122.

4. Ibid.

5. Ibid.

6. Online Bible, Barnes, accessed 17 May 2010.

7. Vine, vol. 2, 524.

8. Ibid., 495.

9. Ibid., 252.

10. Ibid., 496.

11. William Brooks and Robert W. Heath, *Speech Communication* (Madison, WI: WBC Brown and Benchmark, 1993), 80.

12. Vine, vol. 2, 414.

13. Ibid., 568.

14. Ibid., 583.

15. Ibid., 131-132.

16. J. R. Harris, Ed., Gleason L. Archer, Jr., asst. ed., and Bruce K. Waltke, asst. ed., *Theological Wordbook of the Old Testament.* Vol. 1, 2 (Chicago: Moody Press, 1980), vol. 2, 742.

17. _____, *Light for My Path* (Unionville, OH: Barbour Publishing Co., 1999), 13.

18. Sherry Langton, "One Woman's Story," *Today's Christian Woman*, Jan/Feb, 1996, 43-46.

19. Dr. Susan Forward, Joan Torres, *Men Who Hate Women and the Women that Love Them* (Toronto: Bantam Books, 1986), 50.

20. Elisabeth Elliot, *Let Me Be A Woman* (Wheaton, IL: Tyndale House Publishers, Inc., 1976), 25.

21. Harris, vol. 2, 660.

22. Ibid., 661.

23. Online Bible, accessed 3 December 2008.

24. Ibid.

25. Ibid.

26. Ibid., accessed 8 October 2007.

27. Ibid.

28. Harris, vol. 1, 80.

29. Ibid., 217-218.

30. Elliot, 31-32.

31. Ibid., 52.

32. Online Bible, *Matthew Henry's Concise Commentary*, accessed 17 August 2008.

33. Harris, vol. 1, 101.

34. Vine, vol. 1, 130.

35. Ibid.

36. Harris, vol. 1, 417.

37. *Webster's Clear Type Dictionary* (Nashville, TN: Thomas Nelson, Inc., 1976), 219.

38. Vine, vol. 1, 25.

39. Ibid., 26.

40. Ibid., vol. 1, 117-118.

41. Maryjane Hooper Tonn, ed., *A Mother is Love* (Milwaukee: Ideals Publishing Corp., 1976), no date.

42. Harris, vol. 1, 326.

43. Webster, 131.

44. Elizabeth George, *Beautiful in God's Eyes* (Eugene, OR.: Harvest House Publishers, 1998), 87-109.

45. Ibid., 109.

46. Webster, 63.

47. Larry Burkett, *"The World's Easiest Guide" to Finances* (Chicago: Northfield Publishing, 2000), 34.

48. Ibid., 31.

49. Webster, 91.

50. Ibid.

51. Emilie Barnes, *Welcome Home* (Eugene, OR.: Harvest House Publishers, 1997), 74.

52. Harris, vol. 2, 877.

53. Ibid.

54. Ibid.

55. Ibid.

56. Ibid.

57. Ibid., 697.

58. Ibid., vol. 2, 547.

59. Vine, vol. 1, 291.

60. Ibid., 743.

61. Ibid.

62. Ibid.

63. Ibid., 742.

64. Ibid.

65. Harris, vol. 1, 534.

66. Vine, vol. 2, 606.

67. Ibid.

68. Online Bible, accessed 5 August, 2008.

69. Ibid., 401.

70. Ibid.

71. Ibid.

72. Ibid.

73. Ibid.

74. Ibid., 503.

75. Ibid., 131-132.

76. Ibid., 213.

77. Ibid., 113.

78. Harris, vol. 1, 188.

79. Ibid., 97.

80. Ibid.

81. Harris, vol. 2, 860.

82. Online Bible, accessed 5 August 2008.

83. Ibid., Matthew Henry's Concise Commentary, accessed 15 November 2010.

84. "Headed for Divorce?", *Gaston Gazette*, 15 January 1993, sec. D, p. 1.

85. Vine, vol. 2, 322.

86. Ibid., 62.

87. Online Bible, Jamieson, Fausset, and Brown, accessed 5 August 2008.

88. Harris, vol. 1, 101.

89. Online Bible, Barnes, accessed 5 August 2008.

90. Ibid., accessed 19 May 2010.

91. Ibid., accessed 5 August 2008.

92. Ibid., accessed 18 May 2010.

93. Ibid., accessed 13 July 09.

94. Dr. Charles L. Surrett, pastor, sermon preached at Emmanuel Baptist Church, Kings Mountain, Mountain, NC, 10 August 2008.

95. Vine, vol. 2, 252.

96. Ibid., 496.

97. Brooks and Heath, 80.

98. Ibid., 87.

99. Vine, vol. 2, 414.

100. Ibid., 568.

101. Online Bible, Trency, accessed 20 July 2009.

102. Gastonia, NC Policeman, *Gaston Gazette*, 1 July 1993.

103. Vine, vol. 2, 583.

104. Ibid.

105. Vine, vol. 2, 131-132.

106. Online Bible, Barnes, accessed 5 August 2008.

107. Online Bible, accessed 21 July 09.

108. Ibid., accessed 20 July 09.

109. Ibid., accessed 21 July 09.

110. Ibid., accessed 20 July 09.

111. Ibid.

112. Online Bible, Jamieson, Fausset, and Brown, accessed 7 July 2009.

113. Ibid., accessed 26 July 09.

114. Ibid.

115. James Schaffer, Colleen Todd, *Christian Wives–Women Behind the Evangelists Reveal Their Faith in Modern Marriage* (Garden City, NY: Doubleday, 1987), n. d.

116. Webster, 178.

117. Ibid., 352, 484.

118. Ibid., 108.

119. Harris, vol. 1, 259-260.

120. Vine, vol. 2, 381.

121. Ibid., 606.

122. Harris, vol. 1, 188.

123. Vine, vol. 2, 230.

124. Harris, vol. 1, 101.

125. Ibid., 102.

126. Ibid., vol. 2, 930.

127. Elliot, 31-32.

www.ingramcontent.com/pod-product-compliance
Lightning Source LLC
Chambersburg PA
CBHW080444110426
42743CB00016B/3277